D0771957

INNcredible Edibles

INNcredible Edibles

Recipes from Colorado's Hotel Chefs

Colorado Hotel & Lodging Association
Denver, Colorado

The recipes contained in this publication have been given with permission from the hotel chefs, innkeepers, owners, and directors of the properties listed.

©1999 Colorado Hotel & Lodging Association
All Rights Reserved

Published by Colorado Hotel & Lodging Association
999 18th Street, Suite 1240, Denver, Colorado 80202

Cover photography and design layout by
Barbara Batt - BattDesign
Crested Butte, Colorado

Printed in the United States of America

Colorado Hotel & Lodging Association
INNcredible Edibles compiled by Jean Marie Martini
and edited by Ilene Kamsler

p. cm.

Library of Congress Catalogue
Card Number 99 076189

ISBN 0-9676400-0-8
1 3 5 7 9 10 8 6 4 2
First Edition

Table of Contents

Breakfast

South Western Eggs Fiesta

12 individual soufflé dishes (5 - 8 ounce)
24 Eggs
(12) 1 ounce cheddar cheese slices
bacon bits or crumbled cooked turkey bacon
sour cream
mild picante sauce
6 snack size flour tortillas
cilantro
parsley for garnish

Serves 12

1. Grease souffle dishes with non-stick spray and break two eggs into each dish.
2. Slice tortillas in half and place in dishes with flat edge down and outside eggs to form a U-shape around outer edge of dish.
3. Top with 1 ounce slice of cheddar cheese and crumbled bacon or bacon bits and sprinkle with a dash of cilantro.
4. Bake at 375 degrees for 30 minutes or until eggs are done, cheese is melted and tortilla is slightly brown.
5. Top with a dab of sour cream and a teaspoon of picante sauce.
6. Sprinkle a dash of cilantro on top and serve on a plate. Garnish with parsley if desired.

Holden House 1902 Bed & Breakfast Inn
Colorado Springs

Eggs and Sausage Casserole

Serves 9

1 pound Bob Evans "Blue Sage Dressing" sausage or favorite sage sausage
9 eggs, beaten
3 cups milk
1 1/2 teaspoon salt
1 1/2 teaspoon dry mustard
1 1/2 cups shredded cheddar cheese
9 slices of bread, crust removed, torn into small pieces

This dish should be prepared the night before serving.

1. Mix eggs and milk, beat well.
2. Add salt, dry mustard, cheddar cheese, and bread pieces. Blend well.
3. Place mixture in a 9" x 13" glass dish.
4. Brown sausage and drain well.
5. Crumble sausage when cool and sprinkle over mixture in glass dish.
6. Refrigerate overnight.
7. Bake at 350 degrees for 45 minutes.
8. Let stand for 15 minutes until firm, cut and serve.

Elk Mountain Guest Ranch
Buena Vista

1-2-3 Coffee Cake

Cake Ingredients:
1 box yellow cake mix
3 eggs
1 can peach pie filling

Topping Ingredients:
1/2 cup flour
1/2 cup sugar
1/4 cup margarine

Serves 8 - 10

1. Beat eggs, cake mix and pie filling together.
2. Spread in greased 9" x 13" pan.
3. Blend crumb topping and sprinkle on cake batter.
4. Bake at 350 degrees for 40 minutes.

Best Western Brush
Brush

Homestyle Colorado Quiche

Serves 8 - 10

Pie Dough Ingredients:

2 cups flour
1 tablespoon sugar
1 tablespoon salt
1/2 pound cold, unsalted butter
1/4 cup vegetable shortening
1/3 cup ice water

Quiche Ingredients:

2 cups heavy cream
3 whole eggs
1/4 teaspoon salt
1/4 teaspoon black pepper
pinch nutmeg
2/3 cup smoked mozzarella, shredded
3/4 buffalo sausage (or your favorite sausage), sliced thin
4 tablespoons fresh basil
2 roma tomatoes
1 pie dough (recipe below)
2 tablespoons butter

1. Prepare pie shell by first mixing flour, sugar and salt.
2. Cut butter into small pieces and add to dry ingredients. Using a knife, chop the butter into pea size pieces. Add vegetable shortening and cut into chunks to disburse throughout the bowl. Continue to chop until mix becomes coarse crumbs. Add ice water. Mix with rubber spatula until evenly moistened. Using your hands press until the dough coheres. Divide in half and press flat and wrap each piece in plastic. Refrigerate at least 30 minutes.
3. Roll one piece and place in pie tin.

Continued on next page

Sunday Brunch
Englewood

4. Sauté sausage in butter. Drain and let cool.
5. Julienne basil.
6. Peel skin off tomatoes and dice medium size.
7. Mix eggs, salt, pepper, nutmeg and whisk together. Add heavy cream. Add shredded mozzarella and sausage to the pie shell. Slowly add in the heavy cream and egg mix.
8. Bake at 350 degrees for 45 minutes (may need to foil tip if turning too brown).
9. Take out of oven and garnish with chopped chives.

Morning Glory Muffins

Makes 24

2 1/2 cups all-purpose flour
1 cup packed brown sugar
2 teaspoons baking soda
2 teaspoons ground cinnamon
1/2 teaspoon salt
2 cups shredded carrot
1 cup shredded rome beauty or other cooking apple
3/4 cup raisins
1/3 cup chopped pecans
1/4 cup flaked sweetened coconut
1 (8 ounce) can crushed pineapple in juice, drained
1/3 cup vegetable oil
1/3 cup apple butter
2 teaspoons vanilla extract
2 large eggs
2 large egg whites
cooking spray

1. Preheat oven to 350 degrees.
2. Lightly spoon flour into dry measuring cups and level with a knife. Combine flour, sugar, baking soda, cinnamon and salt in a large mixing bowl.
3. Stir in carrot, apple, raisins, pecans, coconut and pineapple.
4. Combine vegetable oil, apple butter, vanilla extract, eggs and egg whites and stir with a whisk.
5. Make well in center of flour mixture and add oil mixture, stirring until moist.
6. Spoon batter into 24 muffin cups coated with cooking spray.
7. Bake at 350 degrees for 25 minutes or until muffins spring back when touched lightly in the center.
8. Remove muffins from pans immediately and cool on wire rack.

The Black Forest Bed & Breakfast

The Black Forest Bed & Breakfast
Colorado Springs

Green Chicken Enchilada Casserole

4 chicken breasts
1 medium onion
4 cloves garlic
2 cans cream of chicken soup
2 cans cream of mushroom soup
5 green chili's
8 - 12 ounces Monterey Jack cheese, shredded
8 - 12 ounces Cheddar cheese, shredded
3 dozen corn tortillas
2 tablespoons Canola oil

Serves 6 - 8

1. Bake chicken and reserve the resulting broth. When cool, shred chicken.
2. Chop onion and garlic and saute in canola oil. Add peeled and chopped green chili.
3. When onion is transparent, add soups and chicken broth to make into gravy.
4. Spray 9" x 13" baking dish with spray oil.
5. Tear up corn tortilla and cover bottom of baking dish.
6. Layer some shredded cooked chicken over the tortilla.
7. Combine cheese, add soup mixture, and top with a layer of cheese.
8. Repeat layer process until baking dish is full and finish with a layer of cheese on top.
9. Bake at 350 degrees for 30 minutes and let sit for 5 - 10 minutes before slicing.

Logwood Bed & Breakfast
Durango

Goldminer Muffins

Makes 8 Muffins

1 egg
1/4 cup cooking oil
1/8 cup milk
1 3/4 cups flour
2 1/2 teaspoons baking powder
2 tablespoons sugar

1. Combine oil and milk.
2. Combine flour, baking powder and sugar and add to oil and milk mixture.
3. Pour into muffin pan and bake at 400 degrees for 12 minutes or until tops begin to brown.

Goldminer Hotel
Eldora

Crab Quiche

4 eggs, beaten
1 cup sour cream
1 cup Cheddar and Swiss cheese, mixed
1 can onion rings
1 can crab meat, drained
9" pie crust

Serves 4 - 6

1. Beat eggs and sour cream. Fold in cheese, onion rings and crab meat.
2. Bake pie crust at 350 degrees for 5 minutes. Prick and return to oven for 5 minutes.
3. Pour crab mixture into shell and bake for 35 minutes or until set.

Riversbend Bed & Breakfast
Mancos

Butter-Rich Waffles

Serves 4

2 eggs, separated
1 1/2 cups whole milk
2 tablespoons baking powder, double-acting
1 cup flour
1/2 cup unsalted butter
1/2 cup chopped pecans

1. Preheat waffle iron.
2. In a copper bowl whip egg whites until stiff but not dry and set aside.
3. In a separate bowl, food processor or blender combine the egg yolks, milk, baking powder, flour and melted butter and beat until smooth.
4. Fold in the reserved eggs whites and chopped pecans and bake according to directions for the waffle iron.
5. Serve hot with your favorite toppings or with Apple Cider Syrup (see page 31).

Alps Boulder Canyon Inn
Boulder

Apple French Toast

1/2 cup butter
1 1/2 cups brown sugar
1/2 cup half and half
1 tablespoon cinnamon
3 apples
1 tablespoon lemon juice
8 eggs
2 cups milk
1 loaf french bread

Serves 5

1. Melt butter and combine with 1 cup brown sugar, half and half and cinnamon.
2. Pare and thinly slice apples then sprinkle slices with lemon juice.
3. In a bowl, beat eggs and milk.
4. Slice french bread into 10 slices and place in well-greased jelly roll pan.
5. Pour egg/milk mixture over french bread and top with butter, brown sugar, half and half, cinnamon mixture.
6. Arrange apple slices on top of french bread and sprinkle an additional 1/2 cup brown sugar on top.
7. Bake at 350 degrees for 45 minutes or until puffy and done.
8. May serve with maple syrup, although it tastes great without.

Abriendo Inn
Pueblo

Baked Bacon and Eggs

Serves 4

(5) 4 ounce ramekins
4 slices canadian bacon
8 fresh spinach leaves, washed & patted dry
6 teaspoons butter
1/2 teaspoon dried thyme
4 eggs
pinch of nutmeg
salt and pepper to taste

1. Preheat oven to 325 degrees.
2. In non-stick skillet, lightly brown canadian bacon on both sides and cut into 1/4" pieces.
3. Remove stems from spinach, stack 4 leaves at a time and roll together tightly.
4. Slice diagonally into 1/8" wide slivers (1/2 cup).
5. Place 1 teaspoon butter in each of (4) 4 ounce ramekins and the remaining 2 teaspoons in a fifth ramekin.
6. Place on baking sheet and set in oven for 1 1/2 to 2 minutes to melt, then remove.
7. Set 5th ramekin aside and divide spinach among remaining 4 ramekins. Sprinkle each with a pinch of thyme and top with a piece of bacon.
8. Break an egg into each, sprinkle with nutmeg, salt and pepper, then spoon 1/2 teaspoon of melted butter from 5th ramekin over top.
9. Bake on center rack for 12 - 14 minutes.

Del Norte Café
Del Norte

Tillie's Granola

2 1/2 pounds regular oats
1/2 cup brown sugar
1/2 cup dry milk
1/2 cup coconut
1/4 cup honey
1/4 cup orange juice
1/2 cup Cheerios
1/4 cup raisins

Serves 5 - 6

1. Combine all ingredients and place on cookie sheet.
2. Bake at 250 degrees until golden brown.
3. Serve with fruit and yogurt.

Sylvan Dale Guest Ranch
Loveland

Jennifer's Breakfast Crepes with Mexican Chocolate & Whipped Cream

Serves 12

6 eggs
6 cups milk
3/4 stick melted butter
2 1/2 cups water
1/2 cup rum
6 cups flour
1/2 cup sugar
fresh fruit of your choice
nutmeg

Garnish Ingredients:
Mexican style chocolate
semi-sweet chocolate
cream
powdered sugar
whipped cream

1. Blend or mix ingredients together and let sit for 30 minutes to get all the lumps out.
2. Cook on buttered iron skillet or crepe pan over medium heat until the batter is bubbly all over.
3. Stack crepes on plate until all the batter is cooked.
4. Melt mexican-style chocolate, semi-sweet chocolate and cream on a low burner to make a sauce. Keep warm to use as garnish.
5. Fill crepes with sliced fresh fruit and sprinkle fruit on top to add color. Sprinkle with powdered sugar, chocolate and freshly whipped cream. Dash with nutmeg.

Cottonwood Inn & Gallery
Alamosa

Special Omelet

2 cups potatoes
1/2 cup onion
3 eggs
1 cup cheese, shredded (your favorite)

Serves 2

1. In skillet, fry potatoes and onion.
2. Scramble eggs and add to potatoes.
3. Fold over when firm and place on plate.
4. Sprinkle with shredded cheese and serve.

Add vegetables if you like!

Goldminer Hotel
Eldora

Banana Butterscotch Muffins

Makes 12 Muffins

- 1 cup oatmeal, uncooked quick variety
- 1/2 cup white sugar
- 2 bananas
- 1 cup white all-purpose flour
- 1 teaspoon baking powder
- 1/2 teaspoon baking soda
- 1/2 teaspoon salt
- 1/2 cup butterscotch mini chips
- 1 egg
- 1/4 cup milk
- 1/4 cup vegetable oil
- 1 teaspoon vanilla extract

1. In a food processor, puree oatmeal and sugar until fine; place in mixing bowl with the rest of the dry ingredients.
2. Puree peeled bananas and add to dry mix with other liquid ingredients, stirring by hand just to blend.
3. Fill greased muffin tins 2/3 full and bake in preheated, 400 degree oven for 13 - 15 minutes until the top springs back when lightly touched.

The Baldpate Inn
Estes Park

Fruit Coffee Cake

1 cup margarine
1 3/4 cup sugar
4 eggs
1 teaspoon vanilla
1 teaspoon almond flavoring
3 cups flour
1 1/2 teaspoons baking powder
1 can favorite fruit pie filling

Serves 8

Powdered Sugar Glaze Ingredients:
1/2 cup powdered sugar
1/4 cup water

1. Cream margarine, sugar, eggs, vanilla and almond flavoring
2. Add flour and baking powder.
3. Reserve 1 cup of the dough and spread the remaining dough in an 11" x 15" greased pan.
4. Cover with 1 can fruit pie filling and spoon on the reserved dough.
5. Bake at 350 degrees for 35 - 40 minutes.
6. Drizzle powdered sugar glaze over top.

Best Western Brush
Brush

Ruffled Crepes Isabel

Serves 12

Crepes Ingredients:
1 1/4 cups flour
2 tablespoons sugar
pinch salt
3 eggs
1 1/2 cup milk
2 tablespoons melted butter
1 teaspoon lemon extract (optional)

Egg Mixture Ingredients:
1 1/2 cups milk
1/2 teaspoon salt
1/4 teaspoon pepper
1 tablespoon flour

6 slices cooked turkey bacon (crumbled)
sharp cheddar cheese
sour cream for garnish
fresh dill, parsley or tarragon garnish

1. Blend or mix all crepe ingredients well and let rest for approximately 5 minutes.
2. Make 5 inch crepes using either a well greased skillet or crepe maker.
3. Mix together all egg mixture ingredients except bacon and cheese.
4. Generously grease 24 muffin tins with non-stick spray and press crepes into tins, lightly ruffling edges but being careful not to tear crepes.

Continued on next page

Holden House 1902 Bed & Breakfast Inn
Colorado Springs

5. Place a small square of cheese in bottom of tin and pour egg mixture carefully into each muffin tin, filling just to below top of rim.
6. Top with crumbled bacon.
7. Bake at 375 degrees for 15 - 20 minutes or until mixture is firm and crepes are just lightly brown.
8. Let cool slightly and carefully loosen crepe cups from muffin tins with a fork or knife, taking care not to break crepe edges.
9. Remove from tins with a spoon, place 2 on each plate and top with a small dollop of sour cream and chopped fresh dill, parsley or tarragon.

Rojas Huevos Enchiladas

Serves 5

1/2 cup chopped red bell pepper
(1) 8 ounce package cream cheese
1/2 cup salsa
1 teaspoon salt
1/2 cup chopped onion
10 eggs scrambled and seasoned
10 flour tortillas (7 or 8 inch)
1 1/2 cups shredded Monterey Jack cheese
chopped tomatoes and green onion tops

This dish should be prepared the night before serving.

1. Place pepper, cream cheese, salsa, salt and onion in a blender and blend until smooth.
2. Combine 3/4 cup of the blended mixture with the scrambled eggs.
3. Place 1/3 cup of egg mixture down the center of each tortilla, roll and place seam down in 2 lightly greased 11" x 17" pans.
4. Spoon the remaining sauce over the enchiladas, cover with foil and refrigerate overnight.
5. Bake at 350 degrees for 25 minutes.
6. Sprinkle with cheese and bake another 5 minutes.
7. Garnish with tomatoes and green onion tops.
8. Serve with additional salsa.

Abriendo Inn
Pueblo

Apple Cider Syrup

1 cup apple juice
1 / 2 cup sugar
4 teaspoons corn starch
4 tablespoons butter
1 teaspoon cinnamon, ground

Serves
4

1. Mix apple juice, sugar and corn starch in a heavy sauce pan over medium heat, stirring frequently with a wire whisk until slightly thickened.
2. Add butter and cinnamon and stir until well mixed.
3. If syrup becomes too thick it can be reduced by adding apple juice.

Alps Boulder Canyon Inn
Boulder

Pearl Street Inn French Toast

Serves 6

1 stick butter
1 1/4 cup brown sugar
1 tablespoon water
3 granny smith apples
cinnamon to taste
1/2 cup raisins
1 loaf french bread or homemade white, sliced 1 1/2" thick
1 1/2 cup milk
1/2 cup half and half
1/2 teaspoon salt
7 eggs
1 teaspoon vanilla
nutmeg to taste
sliced almonds

Cream Topping Ingredients:
1/2 cup whipping cream
1/2 cup nonfat plain yogurt
1/4 cup sugar
1/2 teaspoon almond extract

1. Combine butter, brown sugar, and water in a saucepan. Heat on medium until bubbling, stirring frequently.
2. Place in a 9" x 13" pan and allow to cool for 25 - 30 minutes.
3. Peel, core and thinly slice apples. Place in rows, close together and overlapping on top of sauce in pan.
4. Sprinkle with the cinnamon and raisins.
5. Place the slices of bread on top of the apples.
6. Mix milk, eggs, vanilla, salt and pour over the bread. Sprinkle with nutmeg.

Continued on next page

Pam's Restaurant
Boulder

7. Cover and refrigerate for a minimum of 3 hours (overnight is preferable).
8. Bake in 350 degree oven for approximately 60 minutes or until golden brown and crispy.
9. Serve upside down and top with cream topping and sliced almonds.

Blueberry Streusel Cake

Serves 12 - 15

1/3 cup margarine
3/4 cup sugar
1 cup sour cream
2 eggs
1/2 teaspoon vanilla
1 1/4 teaspoons baking powder
1/4 teaspoon salt
1/4 teaspoon baking soda
1 3/4 cups flour
1 1/2 cups canned blueberries

Topping Ingredients:
1/2 cup flour
1/2 teaspoon cinnamon
1/4 cup brown sugar
1/4 cup margarine

1. Preheat oven to 350 degrees.
2. Cream the butter and sugar together.
3. Add wet ingredients and stir.
4. Add dry ingredients, stir and pour into a greased spring-form pan.
5. Cover the batter with blueberries.
6. Combine topping ingredients by cutting in the margarine until the consistency of fine crumbs.
7. Sprinkle the topping over the blueberries.
8. Bake for 40 minutes or until a cake tester inserted into the middle comes out clean.

North Fork Guest Ranch
Shawnee

to:

Two Sisters Lemony Babycakes

Serves 6

1 cup flour
1 teaspoon baking powder
1/2 teaspoon nutmeg
1/4 teaspoon salt
2 eggs, slightly beaten
1 cup low-fat cottage cheese, mashed smooth
3 tablespoons sugar
2 tablespoons lemon zest, finely chopped
2 tablespoons fresh lemon juice
1/3 cup milk

Cranberry Port Sauce Ingredients:
12 ounce bag cranberries (fresh or frozen)
1/2 cup sugar
1 cup ruby port
1 teaspoon vanilla
1 tablespoon butter

1. In a large bowl, stir together dry ingredients and set aside.
2. In a medium bowl, mix eggs and cottage cheese together until combined, then stir in sugar, lemon zest and juice, and milk.
3. Stir egg mixture into dry ingredients until just blended.
4. Heat a non-stick griddle until hot. Spoon a scant 2 tablespoon batter onto griddle for each pancake and cook until barely golden on the bottom. Turn gently and cook until the other side is golden (about 1 minute each side).
5. Serve immediately or keep warm in 200 degree oven. Serve 5 pancakes per plate topped with hot Cranberry Port Sauce and sprinkle with marigold petals.
6. In heavy saucepan, combine cranberries, sugar and Port. Simmer for approximately 15 minutes or until cranberries burst and mixture thickens. Add vanilla and butter and simmer an additional 1 or 2 minutes until butter melts and flavors blend.

Two Sisters Inn
a bed and breakfast

Two Sisters Inn - a bed & breakfast
Manitou Springs

Apple Cinnamon Baked French Toast

Serves 8 - 10

1 large french bread loaf, sliced 1 1/2" or cubed
4 extra-large eggs
3 1/3 cups milk
1 cup sugar
1 tablespoon vanilla
3 teaspoons cinnamon
1 teaspoon nutmeg
6 medium apples, cooking, peeled & cored, sliced
1/8 stick butter

This dish must be prepared the night prior to serving.

1. Spray 9" x 13" glass pan with oil or non-stick spray.
2. Place bread in pan.
3. Combine eggs, 1/2 cup sugar, milk, vanilla and beat.
4. Pour 1/2 of the mixture over the bread, then place the apples slices on top until covered.
5. Pour remaining egg/ milk mixture evenly over apples.
6. Mix 1/2 cup sugar with cinnamon and nutmeg and sprinkle evenly over apples.
7. Dot with butter, cover and refrigerate overnight.
8. Bake, uncovered, in oven preheated to 350 degrees for 1 hour.
9. Allow to rest for 5 - 10 minutes before cutting. Cut into squares and serve with heated syrup.

Uncompahgre Bed & Breakfast
Montrose

Pumpkin Bread

3 cups sugar
1 cup corn oil
4 eggs, beaten
1 can pumpkin or fresh if available
3 cups flour
1 teaspoon baking powder
2 teaspoons baking soda
2 teaspoons nutmeg
2 teaspoons cinnamon
2/3 cup water
1 cup sliced pecans

Makes 2 Loaves

1. Combine sugar, oil and eggs.
2. Add pumpkin and water.
3. Blend with mixer.
4. Add dry ingredients a little at a time, beat well after each addition.
5. Pour into 2 greased and floured loaf pans.
6. Bake at 350 degrees for 1 hour.

You may wish to cut nutmeg and cinnamon to 1 teaspoon each and add 1/2 teaspoon cloves and 1 teaspoon allspice.

Logwood Bed & Breakfast
Durango

Royal Scones

Makes 34 Scones

3 1/2 cups all-purpose flour
3/4 cup sugar
2 1/2 teaspoons baking powder
1/2 teaspoon baking soda
3/4 cup butter, softened
3/4 cup currants soaked in liqueur
(Cream Sherry is our favorite)
1 cup buttermilk

1. Preheat oven to 425 degrees.
2. In a large bowl, stir together flour, sugar, baking powder, soda, and salt until thoroughly blended.
3. Using a pastry cutter, cut butter into flour mixture until it resembles coarse cornmeal.
4. Stir in currants.
5. Make a well in the center of the flour mixture and add buttermilk. Stir with fork until the dough pulls away from the side of the bowl. Gather dough into a ball and put on a lightly floured board and knead in another 1/2 cup flour if necessary to make a firm biscuit dough.
6. Roll or pat into a circle about 1/2" thick and, using a small heart-shaped or daisy-shaped cookie cutter, cut into individual scones.
7. Place 1 1/2" apart on lightly greased baking sheets.
8. Lightly sprinkle on a mixture of cinnamon and sugar.
9. Bake for 20 - 30 minutes or until tops are lightly brown and the scones are firm to touch.

Castle Marne Bed & Breakfast
Denver

South of the Border Potatoes

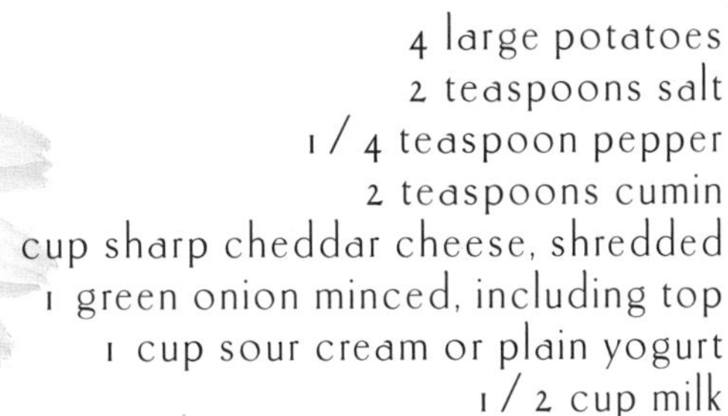

4 large potatoes
2 teaspoons salt
1/4 teaspoon pepper
2 teaspoons cumin
1 cup sharp cheddar cheese, shredded
1 green onion minced, including top
1 cup sour cream or plain yogurt
1/2 cup milk

Serves 5 - 6

This dish should be prepared the night before serving.

1. Bake potatoes and cut into 1 1/2 inch cubes after they have cooled. (Do not remove skins)
2. Mix with the salt, pepper, cumin, cheddar cheese and green onions.
3. Combine sour cream and milk and mix into the rest of the ingredients.
4. Put potato mixture in a well greased 9" x 11" pan and refrigerate overnight.
5. Bake in oven preheated to 375 degrees for 45 minutes.

Abriendo Inn
Pueblo

The I Can't Bake Chocolate Chip Banana Nut Bran Muffin

Serves 4 - 6

(1) 6.4 ounce Gold Medal banana nut muffin mix
1/3 cup milk
1 tablespoon vegetable oil
1 egg
1 ripe banana
1/4 cup bran
1/4 cup Nestles semi-sweet chocolate chip mini morsels

1. Preheat oven to 425 degrees.
2. Beat eggs, milk and oil in small mixing bowl.
3. Add banana and mash into egg mixture.
4. Stir in muffin mix, then stir in bran and chocolate chips.
5. Bake 20 minutes or until golden brown.

Del Norte Café
Del Norte

Mt. Elbert Rhubarb Muffins

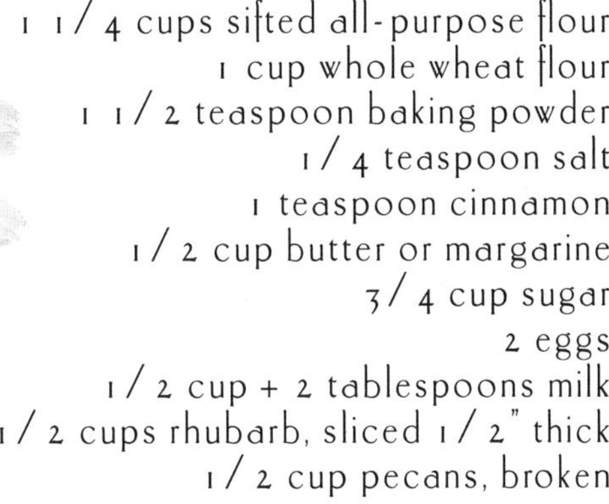

1 1/4 cups sifted all-purpose flour
1 cup whole wheat flour
1 1/2 teaspoon baking powder
1/4 teaspoon salt
1 teaspoon cinnamon
1/2 cup butter or margarine
3/4 cup sugar
2 eggs
1/2 cup + 2 tablespoons milk
2 1/2 cups rhubarb, sliced 1/2" thick
1/2 cup pecans, broken

Makes 12 Muffins

1. Preheat oven to 425 degrees. Grease muffin pan well.
2. Sift flour, baking powder, salt and cinnamon.
3. Cream butter and sugar until light and fluffy. Add eggs one at a time, beating until well blended.
4. Add flour mixture alternately with milk, beating by hand until just combined.
5. Fold in rhubarb and pecans.
6. Fill muffin cups about 2/3 full and sprinkle with sugar.
7. Bake 20 - 30 minutes until golden brown. Cool slightly in pan before serving.

Mount Elbert Lodge
Twin Lakes

Sour Cream Coffee Cake

Serves 8 - 10

Batter Ingredients:
3/4 cup butter, softened
1 1/2 cups sugar
3 eggs
1 1/2 teaspoon vanilla
3 cups all-purpose flour
1 1/2 teaspoon baking powder
1 1/2 teaspoon baking soda
1 1/2 teaspoon salt
1 1/2 cups sour cream

Filling Ingredients:
1/2 cup brown sugar
1/2 cup finely chopped walnuts
1/2 teaspoon cinnamon

1. Preheat oven to 350 degrees. Grease 10" x 14" pan.
2. Mix filling ingredients and set aside.
3. Combine butter, sugar, eggs and vanilla in a large mixing bowl. Beat on medium speed for 2 minutes.
4. Mix in flour, baking powder, soda and salt alternately with sour cream.
5. Spread 1/3 of batter in pan and sprinkle with 1/3 of the filling. Repeat until all batter is used.
6. Bake for approximately 60 minutes, checking at 50 minutes. Insert a toothpick into the center of the cake to test. If the toothpick comes out clean, the cake is done.
7. Cool and serve.

C Lazy U Ranch
Granby

Blueberry Muffins

2 cups flour
2/3 cup sugar
1 tablespoon baking powder
1/2 teaspoon salt
2 eggs
1 cup milk
1/3 cup margarine, melted
1 teaspoon nutmeg
1 teaspoon vanilla
1 cup blueberries
Sugar/cinnamon mixture

Makes 16 Muffins

1. Combine flour, sugar, baking powder and salt.
2. In separate bowl, beat eggs. Blend in milk, margarine, nutmeg and vanilla.
3. Pour egg mixture into dry ingredients and mix until moistened. Fold in blueberries (if blueberries are frozen, rinse and toss in a small amount of flour before adding to batter).
4. Spray muffin tins with vegetable spray and fill 2/3 full.
5. Bake at 375 degrees for 25 minutes or until lightly browned.
6. Brush tops with melted margarine and sugar/cinnamon mixture.

Waunita Hot Springs Ranch
Gunnison

Crumb Coffee Cake

Makes 3 Cakes

3 cups flour
2 sticks margarine
2 1/2 cups sugar
1 teaspoon nutmeg
1 teaspoon cinnamon
2 cups buttermilk
2 eggs
1 teaspoon cloves
1/2 teaspoon salt
2 teaspoons baking soda
optional: nuts and raisins

1. Mix flour, margarine, and sugar until crumbly.
2. Mix remaining ingredients and combine with flour 1/4 cup of the flour mixture.
3. Pour into 3 cake pans and sprinkle with reserved 3/4 cup of crumbs.
4. Bake at 350 degrees for 30 - 40 minutes.

Note: If baking in aluminum pans, place pans on cookie sheet for even baking.

Old Town GuestHouse
Colorado Springs

Breakfast Casserole

12 slices bread (a mixture of white, rye, sour dough or pumpernickel)
2 - 3 cups cooked breakfast meat (ham, sausage or crumbled bacon)
6 large eggs, beaten
2 cups half and half
8 - 12 ounces grated cheddar cheese
1 small onion
1/2 green pepper
1 tablespoons Canola oil
Mrs. Dash seasoning

Serves 6 - 8

This dish should be prepared the night before serving.

1. Chop onion, pepper and saute in Canola oil until limp.
2. Cube bread.
3. Spray a 9" x 13" baking dish with spray cooking oil.
4. Spread bread in bottom of baking dish.
5. Layer ingredients: meat, onion, pepper, and cheese.
6. Combine beaten eggs and half and half, blend and pour over layered mixture.
7. Shake Mrs. Dash over top.
8. Cover and refrigerate overnight.
9. Bake at 350 degrees for 40 - 50 minutes until brown on top. Let sit for 5 minutes before serving.

Logwood Bed & Breakfast
Durango

Blueberry Smoothie

Serves 1

1 ripe medium banana
3/4 cup fresh or frozen blueberries
1/4 cup nonfat vanilla yogurt
3/4 cup skim milk
pinch of cinnamon
1/2 cup crushed ice

1. Combine all ingredients in a blender and puree until smooth.

You may substitute any other fruit to create new smoothies.

North Fork Guest Ranch
Shawnee

Banana-Oatmeal Pancakes with Apple Topping

3/4 cup quick cooking rolled oats
2/3 cup whole wheat flour or home ground triticale or wheat
1 teaspoon baking powder
1/2 teaspoon baking soda
1 tablespoon sugar
1/4 teaspoon salt (optional)
1 medium sized ripe banana
1 egg
1 1/4 cup lowfat buttermilk
2 tablespoons salad oil
3 cups panfried apple slices with cinnamon

Serves 3 - 4

1. Combine oats, flour, baking powder, baking soda, sugar and salt.
2. In a blender, whirl banana with egg and buttermilk; stir into dry ingredients, blending well.
3. Cook 3" diameter pancakes in non-stick pan, 2 minutes on one side, 1 1/2 minutes on the second side.
4. Serve with apples and cinnamon. Dust with powdered sugar if desired.

Uncompahgre Bed & Breakfast
Montrose

German Puff Pancakes with Spiced Apples

(12) 12 ounce individual souffle serving bowls
(High temperature oven-proof)

Egg Mixture Ingredients:
1 1/2 cups flour
Serves 12
1 1/2 cups milk
9 eggs
3 teaspoons vanilla

Apple Mixture Ingredients:
7 medium apples (any variety-mixed green & red is more attractive)
3/4 cup brown sugar
1 teaspoon each: cinnamon, nutmeg, ginger
1/2 cup mincemeat (dried condensed/canned)
4 tablespoons butter/margarine
1/4 cup water

12 pats of butter/margarine
ground nutmeg for garnish
whipped topping for garnish
12 sliced apple wedges for garnish

1. Whip milk, flour, eggs and vanilla and set aside.
2. Place pat of butter in each bowl then preheat bowls in 400 degree oven for 10-15 minutes or until butter is popping hot.
3. While bowls preheat, cut apples into chunks and place in fry pan with butter. Cook for 15 minutes or until apples are moderately soft. Add a bit of water if apples become too dry while cooking.

Continued on next page

Holden House 1902 Bed & Breakfast Inn
Colorado Springs

4. Once cooked, add cinnamon, nutmeg, ginger, brown sugar and mincemeat to apples. Continue cooking another 5 - 10 minutes or until well mixed and hot.
5. When butter bowls are piping hot, add an even measurement of pancake batter to each dish. Place dishes back in oven. Turn oven up to 425 degrees for 10 minutes then back down to 400 degrees for another 5 minutes or until pancakes are puffed up and slightly brown on edges.
6. Remove from oven, place an even measure of apples in center of each pancake. Top with dollop of whipped topping and sprinkle with fresh nutmeg. Place a wedge of apple on top as garnish and serve on a cloth doily on plate. Be careful! These are extremely hot and may crack plates if doilies are not used.

Savory Ham and Sweet Potato Purses

Serves 6

1 large sweet potato or yam, peeled & chunked (2 cups)
1 tablespoon oil
1/2 large onion, chopped (1/2 cup)
1 large garlic clove, peeled & diced
2 shallots, peeled & diced
3/4 teaspoon dried basil
1 cup mushrooms, sliced (1/4 pound)
1/2 cup red pepper, chopped
1 small tomato, chopped, seeded & drained
1/2 teaspoon celery salt
2 teaspoons fresh lemon juice
1 sheet frozen puff pastry dough, thawed
6 slices Jones Dairy Farm Ham slices (or similar product)
1/2 cup Monterey Jack cheese w/ Jalapeno peppers, grated
1 egg, slightly beaten
optional garnish: diced red, orange, & yellow peppers & parsley

1. In a saucepan, cover sweet potatoes with water and bring to a boil over high heat. Reduce heat to medium and cook until tender (about 15 minutes).
2. Drain, transfer to a mixing bowl and mash coarsely.
3. Heat oil in sauté pan over medium heat. Add onion, garlic, shallots and basil and sauté for 2 minutes. Add mushrooms and red pepper and cook for about 7 minutes or until mushroom liquid has evaporated.
4. Add sautéed vegetables, tomato, celery salt and lemon juice to the sweet potatoes and combine gently. (Filling may be covered and refrigerated overnight at this point. Remove from refrigerator and allow to warm slightly before proceeding.)
5. Preheat oven to 400 degrees.

Continued on next page

Two Sisters Inn
a bed and breakfast

Two Sisters Inn - a bed & breakfast
Manitou Springs

6. Lay sheet of pastry dough on floured surface and cut into thirds lengthwise, then cut each third in half crosswise. Roll out into (6) 6-inch squares.
7. Center 1 slice of ham on each square. Spoon 1/6 of filling onto each square, top with a generous tablespoon of cheese, then pull the corners of each square up and twist to secure. Flare out corners to resemble a purse.
8. Brush beaten egg over purses and place on ungreased baking pan.
9. Bake for 30 minutes until golden and serve immediately, garnished with pepper "jewels" and parsley.

Lemon Cheese Filled Pastry

Serves 24

Filling Ingredients:
16 ounces cream cheese, softened
3/4 cup sugar
1 teaspoon vanilla
3 tablespoons lemon juice from fresh lemon
1 teaspoon lemon peel, grated
2 egg yolks

Dough Ingredients:
2 cups flour
1/2 teaspoon baking soda
1 teaspoon salt
3/4 cup butter
1 cup sugar

1. Cream together cream cheese, sugar, vanilla, lemon juice and peel, and egg yolks. Cheese mixture may be prepared a day in advance, covered and refrigerated.
2. To prepare dough, combine flour, baking soda and salt.
3. In a separate bowl cream together butter and sugar then mix in dry ingredients. Dough should be crumbly.
4. Press 3 cups of dough into bottom of greased 9" x 13" pan.
5. Bake at 350 degrees for 8 minutes.
6. Spread cheese mixture over top of baked crust and sprinkle remaining crumb mixture on top of cheese and bake for at least 30 minutes.
7. Cool and cut into 24 portions.

The Anniversary Inn
Bed & Breakfast
Where every day is a special occasion

The Anniversary Inn
Estes Park

Yeast-Raised Pancakes

1 1/2 cups flour
1/2 cup whole wheat flour
3/4 teaspoon salt
1 packet active dry yeast
2 tablespoons sugar
1/2 cup warm water
1 1/2 cups milk, warmed
3 tablespoons butter
2 eggs

Makes 12 Pancakes

1. Whisk flours and salt then set aside.
2. Melt butter in warmed milk.
3. Combine flour mixture, yeast, and milk/butter mixture.
4. Add eggs to batter prior to frying on griddle.

Old Town GuestHouse
Colorado Springs

Lemon Poppy Seed Bread

Makes 1 Cake

1 lemon cake mix
1 small package lemon instant pudding
4 eggs
1/2 cup oil
1 cup water
1/4 cup poppy seeds

1. Mix all ingredients and pour in bundt cake pan.
2. Bake at 350 degrees for 45 minutes.

Best Western Brush
Brush

Key-sch Supreme

1 unbaked pie crust, 9"
8 ounces Swiss cheese, shredded
4 eggs
1 tablespoon white flour
1/2 teaspoon salt
dash of nutmeg
1 cup heavy whipping cream
1 cup light cream (half & half)

Serves 6 - 8

1. Spread cheese evenly in unbaked crust.
2. Mix remaining ingredients together and pour over cheese. Bake at 375 degrees for 40 - 60 minutes until light golden brown and set. A table knife inserted near the center should come out cleanly.
3. Remove from oven. Key-sch may fall slightly after coming out of oven - don't worry it still tastes great!
4. Serve warm with fresh fruit garnish and crispy bacon.

The Baldpate Inn
Estes Park

Banana Sour Cream Coffee Cake

Makes 1 Cake

1/2 cup shortening
1 1/4 cup sugar
2 eggs
2 ripe bananas, mashed
1/2 teaspoon vanilla
1/2 cup sour cream
2 cups flour, sifted
1 teaspoon baking powder
1 teaspoon baking soda
1/4 teaspoon salt
1/2 cup pecans or walnuts, chopped
1/2 teaspoon cinnamon

1. In a large mixing bowl, cream shortening and 1 cup sugar until light and fluffy. Beat in eggs, banana and vanilla. Stir in sour cream.
2. Sift together flour, baking soda, baking powder and salt and gently fold the creamed mixture by hand, stirring just to blend.
3. In another bowl, mix together nuts, remaining sugar and cinnamon. Sprinkle half the nut mixture into the bottom of a well-greased 6 1/2 cup ring mold, tube or bundt pan. Spoon half the batter over this. Sprinkle with remaining nuts and rest of batter.
4. Bake at 350 degrees for 40 - 45 minutes or until cake tester comes our clean. Let stand in pan on rack for 5 minutes. Loosen around edges and turn out on plate.

Boulder Victoria
Boulder

Upside Down Muffin Pie

Muffin Ingredients:
1/2 cup milk
1 egg
2 tablespoons butter
1/4 cup sugar
baking powder
1/4 teaspoon salt
3/4 teaspoon cake spice
1 cup rounded flour

Serves 4 - 6

Topping Ingredients:
1 apple, cored and sliced
1 tablespoon lemon juice
2 tablespoons butter, melted
1/4 to 1/2 cup brown sugar (depending on your taste)
pecans if desired

1. Mix all muffin ingredients together adding the flour last and set aside.
2. Arrange fruit slices and pecan (if desired) in the bottom of a greased 9" pie pan.
3. In a separate bowl, mix lemon juice, butter and brown sugar. Pour mixture over apples then dollop the muffin mix over brown sugar mixture.
4. Place pie pan on a cookie sheet (to catch any dribbles) and bake at 400 degrees for 30 minutes. Remove from oven and immediately turn upside down on a large plate. Serve warm.

Mount Elbert Lodge
Twin Lakes

Walnut-Caramel French Toast

Serves 8

1 cup brown sugar
1/2 cup butter
2 tablespoons light corn syrup
1 cup walnuts, chopped
8 slices french bread
fresh peaches, sliced
6 eggs
1 1/2 cups milk
1 teaspoon vanilla

Topping Ingredients:
1 cup yogurt
1 cup sour cream

This dish should be prepared the night before serving.

1. Combine brown sugar, butter and corn syrup and cook over medium heat until thickened, stirring constantly.
2. Pour into 9" x 13" pan sprayed with Pam. Sprinkle with walnuts and place a layer of 8 slices of french bread on the syrup and nuts. Top with 3 or 4 peach slices on each piece of bread.
3. In blender, combine eggs, milk and vanilla.
4. Pour 1/2 of egg/milk mixture over the bread and peaches. Place a second layer of bread slices on top of peaches and cover with remaining egg/milk mixutre. Cover with plastic wrap and refrigerate overnight.
5. Bake, uncovered, for 40 - 50 minutes at 350 degrees. Remove from oven and invert on cookie sheet.
6. Combine topping ingredients and spoon over each serving. Top with fresh peaches.

Riversbend Bed & Breakfast
Mancos

Teacakes

20 double graham crackers
1/2 cup walnuts
1/2 cup butter, melted
1 square (1 ounce) unsweetened chocolate
3/4 cup sugar
2 eggs, lightly beaten

Makes 12 - 14 Small Bars

Butter Frosting Ingredients:
3 tablespoons butter
2 1/2 cups powdered sugar
1 teaspoon vanilla
1/8 to 1/4 cup light cream

1. Crush crackers and nuts in a blender or food processor and set aside.
2. Melt butter and chocolate in small saucepan over medium heat.
3. Add sugar and eggs.
4. Let mixture simmer approximately 2 minutes.
5. Remove from heat and add crackers and nuts, mix well.
6. Pat firmly into an ungreased 11" x 17" pan and let cool.
7. Frost with butter frosting and decorate with silver decorettes.

To prepare butter frosting:
1. Cream butter in a medium bowl until fluffy.
2. Slowly add powdered sugar and light cream, alternating until a frosting forms.
3. Add vanilla.

Castle Marne Bed & Breakfast
Denver

Starters:
Appetizers, Salads, Soups, Breads

Wild Mushrooms Ragout in Puff Pastry

Serves 4

1/2 cup Shiitake mushrooms
1/2 cup Portobello mushrooms
1/2 cup Oyster mushrooms
1/2 cup Crimini mushrooms
1 teaspoon shallots, chopped
1 teaspoon garlic, chopped
1 tablespoon Cognac
1 cup heavy cream
1/4 cup veal stock
1 teaspoon chives, chopped
1 teaspoon tarragon, chopped
egg wash (1 egg yolk + 1 tablespoon water)
1 tablespoon butter
1 tablespoon oil
puff pastry - 1 sheet cut into (4) 4" x 3" rectangles
Italian parsley for garnish

1. Place cut puff pastry rectangles on sheet pan with wax paper and brush with egg wash. Make a design with a fork and put in oven for 10 minutes at 375 degrees. Drop the temperature to 250 degrees for 5 more minutes to remove all moisture. When nicely browned, remove and set aside.
2. Sauté the sliced wild mushrooms in sauté pan with oil and butter until they are brown and lose all moisture.
3. Add the chopped garlic and shallots, then flambé with cognac and add heavy cream and veal stock. Reduce slowly until nice consistency. Finish with chives, tarragon, salt and fresh ground whole white pepper.
4. Cut the puff pastry in half. Put the first half on a small plate, put the ragout over it and finish with the other pastry half and garnish with Italian parsley.

The Antlers
Durango

Artichoke Heart Dip

Serves 8

1 pound can artichoke hearts (packed in salt water)
1 cup parmesan cheese
1 cup mayonnaise
3 ounces cream cheese
dry bread crumbs
pat of butter

1. Cut artichokes into small pieces.
2. Mix ingredients together and pour into pan.
3. Mix bread crumbs and butter and sprinkle on top.
4. Bake at 350 degrees until golden brown on top. (Can be baked in a bread bowl.)
5. Serve with Triscuits.

Sylvan Dale Guest Ranch
Loveland

Southwestern White Pizza

(1) 12" flour tortilla
1/4 cup hummus
1 roma tomato, sliced
2 fire roasted anaheim peppers, sliced julienne style
1/4 cup fresh mozzarella cheese

Makes 8 Slices

1. Spread hummus evenly on tortilla.
2. Arrange tomatoes, peppers, and cheese to cover.
3. Bake at 400 degrees 5 - 10 minutes until hot.
4. Remove from oven and cut 8 slices.

Foothills Restaurant
Denver

Swiss Fondue

Serves 2

3/4 cup Gruyere cheese, grated
3/4 cup Emmental cheese, grated
1 1/2 cups dry white wine
1/2 tablespoon garlic
1/4 teaspoon nutmeg
1/4 teaspoon black pepper
1/8 teaspoon cayenne
1 tablespoon corn starch
1 tablespoon Kirschwasser
1 loaf sour dough bread, cut in 1" cubes

1. Place white wine, garlic and spices in a fondue pot. Bring to simmer over high heat, then add the cheeses.
2. Bring to a boil while constantly stirring, then reduce heat to a simmer.
3. In a small glass mix the Kirschwasser and the corn starch. Slowly add this mixture to the fondue, keep stirring during this process.
4. Once it has returned to a boil, serve immediately. Serve the cubed bread on the side for dipping. Keep warm during service using a fondue pot warmer.

Swiss Chalet Restaurant
Vail

Brushetta

6 garlic bulbs (small)
1/3 cup Asiago cheese, shaved
1 cup roma tomatoes, seeded & diced
1 tablespoon fresh basil, chopped
1/8 cup extra virgin olive oil
4 teaspoons garlic, minced
1/4 teaspoon salt
1/4 teaspoon black pepper
6 slices french bread slices, cut 3/4" thick
1 sprig parsley

Serves 6

1. Cut tops off of garlic bulbs and roast at 250 degrees, covered for about an hour or until garlic is roasted throughout. Keep warm.
2. Shave Asiago cheese with vegetable peeler and set aside.
3. Squeeze roasted garlic out of each clove.
4. Combine diced roma tomatoes, basil, olive oil, minced garlic, salt and pepper and mix well.
5. Rub each slice of bread with olive oil and toast.
6. Arrange all ingredients on platter and garnish with parsley sprig.

Caper Bistro
Denver

Zucchini and Feta Frittata

Serves 6 - 8

3 cups zucchini, thinly sliced
salt
2 tablespoons butter
1/4 cup bread crumbs, plain or italian
1/3 cup feta cheese, crumbled
1/2 to 3/4 cup ham, cubed
10 eggs
1/4 cup fresh Parmesan cheese, coarsely grated
14 ounces canned peeled, diced tomatoes, drained

1. Place 1 layer of zucchini slices on sheets of paper towels and sprinkle with salt, then cover with more sheets of paper towel. As the moisture is drawn out of the zucchini and the towels become damp, replace with fresh paper towels. This takes about 30 - 40 minutes, replacing towels 3 - 4 times.
2. Melt butter in a 10" pie plate, tilting to evenly coat bottom and sides.
3. Sprinkle bread crumbs evenly over bottom only. Place zucchini slices on top of crumbs in layers, beginning around the outside and moving toward the center. Sprinkle on feta cheese and ham.
4. Beat eggs until light and frothy and pour gently over the zucchini mix and sprinkle Parmesan on top.
5. Bake at 350 degrees for 35 - 40 minutes. Let cool 10 minutes and cut into 6 or 8 portions.

The Anniversary Inn
Bed & Breakfast
Where every day is a special occasion

Anniversary Inn
Estes Park

Wild Mushroom and Roasted Garlic Pesto

1/2 cup peeled garlic cloves
1/2 cup peeled shallots
2 cups shiitake mushrooms, stemmed & sliced
1 tablespoon oyster sauce
1/4 teaspoon white pepper
1/4 cup red wine
water as needed

Serves 8 - 10

1. Roast garlic and shallots on a flat pan at 350 degrees for 30 - 45 minutes, until dark brown.
2. Combine all other ingredients in a sauté pan and bring to a simmer. Simmer until mushrooms are cooked through and any remaining liquid has achieved a "syrup" consistency. Allow to cool.
3. Place mixture in a food processor with roasted garlic and shallot cloves squeezed out of their skin and puree to a medium consistency. Water or red wine may be added to achieve desired texture.
4. Store under refrigeration or freeze.
5. Serve with bread toasts, crackers or fresh vegetable cruditites as a dip.

Palm Court
Glenwood Springs

Durango Eggrolls

Serves 2

(2) 8" flour tortilla (thin fajita style)
4 tablespoons black bean puree or refried black beans
3 teaspoons canned, frozen or fresh kernel corn
3 teaspoons fresh or frozen chopped leaf spinach
3 teaspoons jalapeno jack cheese, diced
blue corn meal
eggwash (1 egg yolk and 1 tablespoon water)
frying oil (1" deep or in deep fat fryer)

1. Place corn meal in a shallow bowl.
2. Place eggwash in a shallow bowl.
3. Lay out tortilla and spread black bean puree in middle, then add layer of corn, then spinach and finally cheese. Roll the tortilla as you would an eggroll, turning the sides in first, then rolling fairly tightly.
4. Holding the roll together, dip it into the eggwash, then into the corn meal.
5. Lay in a shallow pan, open side down and prepare as many eggrolls as you wish.
6. Refrigerate eggrolls for 1 hour.
7. Deep fry until crispy.
8. Serve immediately with your favorite salsa.

Café Durango
Durango

Royal Flush Sandwich

1/2 pound deli slice lean roast beef
4 slices red steak tomato
4 large leaves bibb or green leaf lettuce
1 avocado, sliced
1/2 cup cranberry horseradish dressing
4 tablespoons mayonnaise
2 large pumpernickel rolls

Serves 2

1. Slice pumpernickel roll and spread mayonnaise on both sides of roll.
2. Place open face on plate and add lettuce to both sides. Place both tomato slices and avocado slices on one side and pile beef high on the other.
3. Serve with ramekin of cranberry horseradish on the side.

Garden Terrace
Colorado Springs

Roasted Garlic Pesto

Serves 8 - 10

4 garlic bulbs (large and firm with large cloves)
1 yellow onion
1/2 cup light olive oil
1/2 teaspoon salt
1/2 teaspoon white pepper
1 pound cooked peeled potatoes

1. Peel off excessive outer skins of garlic bulbs and brush with olive oil. Wrap together in foil.
2. Brush onion with oil and wrap in foil.
3. Bake onion at 275 degrees for 2 1/2 hours.
4. Bake garlic at 275 degrees for 1 1/2 hours.
5. Both onion and garlic should be soft and roasted golden brown.
6. Peel garlic cloves and onion and puree with metal blade in food processor.
7. Slowly drizzle in oil, with processor running, to emulsify.
8. Add seasonings and potato and blend until smooth.
9. Serve with your choice of bread.

COPPER MOUNTAIN RESORT

Pesce Fresco
Copper

Bruschetta with Goat Cheese and Tapenade

Tapenade Ingredients:
1 3/4 cup black olives, finely chopped
1/4 cup chopped sun dried tomatoes
2 tablespoons capers, chopped
1 tablespoon green peppercorns, crushed
4 tablespoons olive oil
2 garlic cloves, crushed
3 tablespoons basil, chopped
salt and pepper to taste

Serves 6

Base Ingredients:
12 slices crusty bread
olive oil for brushing
2 garlic cloves, halved
1/2 cup soft goat cheese
fresh herb sprig garnish

1. Mix all tapenade ingredients together and chill overnight.
2. Broil both sides of bread until golden brown.
3. Brush one side with olive oil.
4. Rub with garlic clove.
5. Spread cheese on bruschetta.
6. Spoon tapenade on top.
7. Garnish and serve.

Top of the World Restaurant
Breckenridge

Sundried Tomato and Pesto Cheese Torte

Serves 4

1/4 cup sundried tomatoes, julienned
1/2 cup ricotta cheese
1/4 cup parmesan cheese
3/4 cup cream cheese
1/2 cup marscapone
1/4 cup pesto

Pesto Ingredients:
1/2 cup basil leaves
2 tablespoons fresh garlic, chopped
1/4 cup parmesan cheese
1/4 cup olive oil
1/4 cup pine nuts

1. Rehydrate tomatoes by placing them in hot water and let stand until soft.
2. Place pesto ingredients in a food processor and mix. (This pesto should be thick to help return it to its shape during the molding and slicing process)
3. Mix the four cheeses until blended thoroughly.
4. In a dish, layer the pesto first, then place cheese mixture and top with sundried tomatoes.
5. Chill until firm.
6. Unmold, slice and serve on a bed of crisp greens.

Best Western Executive Inn
The Cockpit Grille
Denver

Cucumber Appetizers

1 cucumber
1/2 cup angel hair pasta, cooked and chopped
4 tablespoons peanut butter
1 tablespoon soy sauce
1/4 cup peanuts, chopped
1/4 cup green onion, chopped

Serves 4

1. Score outside skin of cucumber and slice into 1/4" slices, discarding end pieces.
2. Mix chopped angel hair pasta with peanut butter and soy sauce to taste.
3. Spoon onto cucumber and garnish with peanuts and green onion.

Uncompahgre Bed & Breakfast
Montrose

Cheese and Bacon in a Bread Boat

1 pound bacon, cooked and diced
1 loaf shepherd's bread
(1) 8 ounce package softened cream cheese
1 cup sour cream
1/2 cup green peppers, chopped
1/2 cup green onions, thinly sliced

Serves 20

1. Crisp bacon and dice in small pieces then set aside.
2. Beat cream cheese and sour cream and add bacon, peppers and onions.
3. Warm filling at 350 degrees for approximately 30 minutes.
4. Hollow out shepherd's bread and save hollowed out pieces.
5. Fill bread with warmed filling and return to oven for 15 - 20 minutes.
6. Serve with extra pieces of bread and a knife to cut bowl.

Elk Mtn Guest Ranch
Buena Vista

Stubé Pine Cone Paté

Serves 8

Foie Gras Paté:
1 pound grade A foie gras
1 tablespoon brandy
1 tablespoon sherry
salt to taste
white pepper to taste

Additional Ingredients:
2 tablespoons pickles, chopped
2 tablespoons capers, chopped
2 tablespoons red onions, small dice
1 cup lingonberry preserves
2 tablespoons pine nuts, roasted
16 pieces small pumpernickel rounds, soaked in kirschwasser
zest of orange for garnish
crushed red pepper flakes for garnish

1. Clean Foie gras (remove veins, blood spots, etc.)
2. Process foie gras in food processor until smooth, then add brandy, sherry, salt and pepper.
3. Pipe paté into pine cone shapes using pastry bag and tip.
4. Place one pine cone on each plate. Arrange pumpernickel slices around the pine cone.
5. Place small amount of gerkins, capers, onions and lingonberry preserves on plate.
6. Garnish lingonberries with orange zest and sprinkle the pine cones with a small amount of red pepper flakes.

Alpenglow Stube
Keystone

Sashimi and Guacamole Terrine with Sesame Seed Vinaigrette

Serves 6

Sashimi Ingredients:

1 pound sashimi grade tuna, 1/4" dice
2 tablespoons wasabi caviar
1/2 bunch cilantro
sweet potato gaufrette chips or tortilla chips

Guacamole Ingredients:

4 avocados (peeled, seeded and diced)
1 cup tomatoes, diced
1 teaspoon garlic, minced
4 tablespoons lemon juice
2 teaspoons cilantro, minced
pinch cayenne pepper
salt and pepper to taste

Sesame Seed Vinaigrette Ingredients:

4 ounces rice wine vinegar
8 ounces sesame seed oil
1 ounce extra virgin olive oil
1 ounce honey
1 teaspoon black sesame seeds, toasted
1 teaspoon white sesame seeds, toasted
pinch ground cumin
pinch curry powder
salt
pepper

1. In food processor, puree 1/2 of the avocados and remove.
2. In mixing bowl, combine avocado puree and remaining ingredients.

Continued on next page

Palace Arms
Denver

3. Gently fold ingredients until mixed.
4. Adjust seasoning and set aside.
5. In a mixing bowl, combine ingredients and mix thoroughly with wire whisk.
6. Adjust seasoning and hold.
7. Using a 3" ring mold, place in middle of plate and evenly distribute guacamole into 6 portions. Place equal amounts of diced tuna on top of guacamole and garnish tuna with caviar. Ladle Sesame Seed Vinaigrette around the terrine. Remove ring mold and place chips equally around the terrine.

Frittata

Serves 1

3 eggs
1 tablespoon water
6 tablespoons seasonal vegetables, small dice
5 slices tomatoes
3 mushrooms
1/4 cup mixed cheeses, grated
1 teaspoon olive oil
1 crusty roll
2 pats butter

1. Heat 10" skillet.
2. Combine eggs and water in mixing bowl and whip.
3. Pour mixture into skillet and as frittata firms, place vegetables, tomatoes, and mushrooms symmetrically on frittata. Sprinkle on cheese and place in melter or under broiler until browned.
4. Serve on warmed plate with roll.

Garden Terrace
Colorado Springs

Stuffed Portobello Mushroom

1 Portobello mushroom (4 - 5" in diameter)
2 heaping tablespoons Feta cheese
1 roma or vine ripe tomato, chopped to 1/4"
1 teaspoon fresh garlic, chopped
1 teaspoon fresh basil, chopped
1 tablespoon extra virgin olive oil
pinch salt
pinch pepper

Serves 1

1. Combine crumbled Feta, garlic, tomato, salt and pepper in a bowl and mix well.
2. Preheat oven to 350 degrees.
3. Break stem off of Portobello and discard. Place mushrooms on an oiled pie pan or cookie sheet.
4. Place Feta mixture on top of mushroom in a uniform layer, drizzle olive oil over the top and sprinkle with Parmesan.
5. Place in oven for 10 - 15 minutes or until top is light browned.

This dish can be prepared several hours in advance.

Palm Court
Glenwood Springs

Campari-Lemon Granita

1 cup Campari liqueur
1 cup white wine
1/4 cup lemon juice
2/3 cup sugar

Serves
2

1. In a small saucepan, over high heat, combine the Campari, wine, lemon and sugar. Bring mixture to boil.
2. Pour Campari mixture into a suitable container for freezing. Place in freezer, stirring with a fork every hour, until set (about 3 hours).
3. Scrape granita into rough chunks and serve in cups or bowls.

Alice's Restaurant
Ward

Curry Cheese Paté

6 tablespoons cream cheese, room temperature
1 cup Sharp Cheddar cheese, shredded
2 teaspoons sherry
1/2 teaspoon curry powder
1/4 teaspoon salt
1/2 cup chutney
1/4 cup green onion, finely chopped

Serves 6

1. Combine cream cheese, sharp cheddar, sherry, curry powder and salt in a food processor and blend until smooth.
2. Spread this mixture in a circular shape about 1/2" thick on a serving plate and chill until firm.
3. Top the cheese mixture with a layer of chutney, leaving an inch circle of exposed cheese. Sprinkle with green onions in center of chutney.
4. Serve with crackers.

Old Town GuestHouse
Colorado Springs

Forest Mushroom with Goat's Beard

Serves 6

Salsify Custard Ingredients:
1 1/2 cups salsify, peeled
1 tablespoon minced shallot
2 teaspoons olive oil
2 teaspoons dijon mustard
2/3 cup white wine
5 teaspoons white pepper
1 teaspoon salt
pinch cayenne
4 tablespoons brandy
2 eggs
2/3 cup heavy cream

Tomato Pedestal Filling Ingredients:
1 teaspoon olive oil
3 tablespoons leek, chopped
1 shallot, minced
2 garlic cloves, minced
1 teaspoon green peppercorns
4 tablespoons champagne vinegar
4 tablespoons tomato juice
1 1/2 cup diced tomato, fresh or canned
4 tablespoons pesto
1/2 teaspoon cracked black pepper
1/2 ounce Asiago cheese, grated
1 tablespoon fresh herbs, minced
3 ounces Stilton cheese puff pastry to wrap

Mushroom Ingredients:
6 small portobello mushrooms
olive oil
balsamic vinegar
salt and pepper

Continued on next page

Keystone Ranch
Keystone

1. Steam the salsify for 20 minutes or until tender and cool.
2. Sauté shallots in oil, deglaze with wine and brandy. Reduce by half and cool.
3. Puree cooled salsify with cooled shallot mixture in food processor along with the remaining custard ingredients.
4. Sauté leek, shallot and garlic in olive oil.
5. Add vinegar, tomato, pesto and pepper. Reduce until nearly dry.
6. Cool and stir in Asiago cheese and herbs.
7. Line mini muffin pans with puff pastry and fill with tomato mixture, then place a bit of Stilton cheese on top of mixture.
8. Bake at 350 degrees for 15 minutes.
9. Remove the stem of the mushrooms and steam the caps. Sprinkle with olive oil, vinegar, salt and pepper, then fill each cap with ample amount of salsify custard and bake on a rack until custard is set. (About 15 minutes at 350 degrees)

Spinach and Pine Nut Phyllo Wrap

Serves 8

1 large yellow onion
1/2 cup olive oil
2 pounds frozen chopped spinach, thawed
3 eggs, lightly beaten
1/2 teaspoon salt
1/2 teaspoon nutmeg
1/2 teaspoon cinnamon
2 tablespoons fine, dry bread crumbs
2/3 cup feta cheese, crumbled
2/3 cup pine nuts
1/2 cup butter
(8) 17" x 12" phyllo sheets
7 tablespoons parmesan cheese, finely grated
1/3 cup fresh parmesan cheese, coarsely grated

1. Sauté onion in olive oil using a large skillet. Cook and stir over medium heat until onion is translucent.
2. Squeeze spinach in a colander, removing as much liquid as possible, and add to onion. Cook until liquid is evaporated, about 2 minutes, and remove from heat. Stir in eggs, salt, nutmeg, cinnamon, bread crumbs and feta cheese.
3. Toast pine nuts in a shallow baking pan at 350 degrees for about 4 minutes. Cool and add to spinach mixture.
4. Melt butter in sauce pan. Place one phyllo sheet on wax paper and brush with 1 tablespoon melted butter. Sprinkle 1 tablespoon finely grated parmesan evenly over buttered sheet and repeat process, layering with 6 more sheets, 6 tablespoons butter, and remaining 6 tablespoons parmesan.
5. Lay sheets in greased 9" x 13" pan, letting excess hang over edge. Spoon in filling, spreading evenly. Fold edges of dough over filling.

Continued on next page

The Anniversary Inn
Bed & Breakfast
Where every day is a special occasion

Anniversary Inn
Estes Park

6. Fold last sheet of phyllo in half and place over top, completely covering filling. Brush with remaining tablespoon of butter and sprinkle with fresh coarsely grated Parmesan.
7. Bake at 350 degrees for 25 - 30 minutes until golden brown.
8. Cut into 8 portions and serve.

Spinach Balls

Serves 5

1 1/8 cup frozen spinach, thawed, drained and chopped
2 eggs
3/4 cup seasoned croutons, blended medium fine
1/4 cup onions, diced
1/4 cup Parmesan cheese
1/4 teaspoon thyme
1/2 teaspoon salt
1/4 teaspoon pepper
1/4 teaspoon garlic powder
1/4 cup margarine, melted

1. Mix all ingredients together and chill.
2. Shape into balls.
3. Bake at 350 degrees for 30 minutes.

Latigo Ranch
Kremmling

Crab Stuffed Mushrooms

3/4 pound crab meat, picked over for shells
1/2 cup plain bread crumbs
1 celery stalk, minced
1 small onion, minced
1 small green pepper, minced
1/2 teaspoon dry mustard
1/2 teaspoon Tabasco
1/2 teaspoon lemon juice
1/2 teaspoon Worcestershire sauce
1/4 cup mayonnaise
16 large mushrooms
4 tablespoons Parmesan, grated
2 tablespoons melted butter

Serves 4

1. Preheat oven to 400 degrees.
2. Combine all ingredients except mushrooms, Parmesan and butter. Blend well.
3. Rinse mushrooms and pat dry. Pull the stems out and fill each cavity with about 1 tablespoon of ctab mixture. Arrange mushrooms in a baking pan, sprinkle with Parmesan and drizzle with melted butter.
4. Bake for 15 minutes or until nicely browned. Serve immediately.

McCormick's Fish House
Denver

Stubé Greens

Serves 8

Champagne Vinaigrette Ingredients:
2 tablespoons dijon mustard
2 egg yolks
1/2 cup sherry vinegar
1/2 champagne vinegar
1 tablespoon fresh ground black pepper
2 tablespoons shallots, minced
1 cup olive oil
1 cup walnut oil
1 cup extra virgin olive oil
1 cup boiling water
1/2 cup champagne

Asiago Cheese Crisp Ingredients:
2 cups Asiago cheese, grated

Greens Ingredients:
12 cups mixed greens
8 roma tomatoes
16 long fresh chives

1. Combine vinaigrette ingredients, excluding champagne, to form an emulsion. Finish with fresh champagne at service.
2. Prepare Asiago Cheese Crisps by melting 1/4 cup of the Asiago cheese in a small teflon pan over medium heat. Cook until cheese melts and turns golden brown on the bottom. Repeat until you have 8 crisps.
3. Flip cheese out onto cutting board and cut in half and mold each half over a wine bottle or rolling pin.

Continued on next page

Alpenglow Stube
Keystone

4. Peel roma tomatoes, slice both ends so they stand up, scoop out each tomato to make a cup, and marinate for 4 hours in the Champagne Vinaigrette.
5. Place 1 tomato cup on each plate and place one cheese crisp around each tomato cup.
6. Place 1 1/2 greens with vinaigrette on each plate flowing from the tomato cup, garnish with chives.

Raspberry Vinaigrette

Makes 3/4 Quart

1/2 cup dijon mustard
1/2 cup raspberry vinegar
1 1/2 tablespoons Herb de Provence
1 cup raspberries
1/2 cup sugar
1/2 teaspoon white pepper
1/2 teaspoon black pepper
1/4 teaspoon salt
1/2 shallot, chopped
1/8 cup walnut oil
1 cup mixed oil (80% vegetable, 20% olive oil)
1 cup olive oil

1. Blend all ingredients, excluding oils, until pureed.
2. With processor running, slowly add oils.
3. Toss with mixed field greens and top with toasted sunflower seeds, bleu cheese crumbles and cherry tomato halves.

Vinaigrette will hold 3 weeks under refrigeration.

Stonebridge Inn Restaurant
Snowmass Village

Black Pepper Potato Bread

2 cups warm water
1 tablespoon honey
1 tablespoon yeast
5 cups all-purpose flour
1 1/2 cups hot mashed potatoes
6 tablespoons butter
2 teaspoons salt
1 1/2 tablespoons black pepper

Makes 2 Loaves

1. In a mixing bowl combine water, yeast and honey. Stir and let stand 5 - 10 minutes. Using a dough hook, begin mixing the dough by adding half the flour to the yeast mixture. Add potatoes, butter and salt. Add black pepper and continue to add flour until the dough is only slightly tacky to the touch.
2. Place dough in a large greased bowl, cover with plastic and place in a warm place to rise.
3. When dough is double in size, about 40 - 60 minutes, divide in half and shape into 2 loaves. Place each loaf in greased loaf pan and let rise again until about 1 - 2" above loaf pan (20 - 40 minutes).
4. Bake at 350 degrees for 25 - 30 minutes. Remove from pans and cool on a rack.

Vista Verde Inn
Steamboat Springs

Warm Hazelnut Vinaigrette

Makes 1 1/2 Quarts

1/4 cup pancetta or bacon, diced small
2 tablespoons red onion, diced small
2 tablespoons hazelnuts, peeled
1 tablespoon celery, diced small
1 cup red wine vinegar
black pepper to taste
1 tablespoon garlic
1/2 cup chablis wine
2 tablespoons brown sugar
1 cup olive oil
salt to taste

1. Roast hazelnuts until golden brown.
2. Sauté pancetta or bacon to render fat, add onion, celery, garlic and sauté for 1 minute.
3. Deglaze pan with Chablis.
4. Add all remaining ingredients and bring to a boil.
5. May need to thicken with a cornstarch slurry.

Sunday Brunch
Englewood

Garden Room Caesar Dressing

1/2 cup red wine vinegar
1/2 cup balsamic vinegar
1 lemon, juice of
1 tablespoon ground black pepper
3 ounce can anchovy fillets
1/4 cup dijon mustard
1/4 cup fresh garlic, minced
3/4 cup pasteurized eggs or 6 whole eggs
1 quart pure olive oil
1 cup grated parmesan cheese

Makes 1 1/2 Quarts

1. Combine vinegars, lemon juice and pepper and reserve.
2. In food processor, combine anchovies, garlic, mustard, eggs and blend well.
3. Slowly add a steady stream of olive oil to egg mixture to make mayonnaise. When mixture gets too thick, thin with vinegar mixture, alternating until all ingredients are combined.
4. Stir in cheese and transfer to plastic container and refrigerate.

The Garden Room
Keystone

Coconut-Fried Chicken Salad with Jalapeño Dressing

Serves
4

4 chicken breasts
3 medium eggs, lightly beaten
1/2 cup bread crumbs
1/2 cup coconut
1/2 cup + 2 tablespoons mixed greens
1 grapefruit, sectioned
1 orange, sectioned
2 red peppers, slice each into 6 rings
2 tomatoes, cut into wedges
1 cup mayonnaise
1/2 cup honey
2 tablespoons jalapenos, diced
1 tablespoon cilantro, chopped

1. To prepare dressing, mix mayonnaise, honey, jalapenos, cilantro and set aside.
2. Bread chicken breasts by combining bread crumbs with coconut. Dip breasts into beaten eggs then into bread crumb mixture until completely coated.
3. Pan-fry chicken until lightly brown and done then reserve.
4. Place lettuce in middle of plate. Alternate citrus sections along top of plate. Slice fried chicken breasts diagonally and place on bottom half of plate. Put 3 pepper rings in center and tomato wedges at 3:00 and 9:00.
5. Drizzle one ounce of dressing onto top and serve.

Aspens
Aurora

Fresh Tuna Nicoise

8 ounces fresh yellowfin tuna steak
5 tiny new red potatoes
15 - 20 young thin green beans
6 - 8 nicoise or kalamata olives
1 small tomato
1/2 small red pepper
1/2 small green pepper
1/4 small red onion
1 hard-boiled egg
salt and pepper to taste
leaf lettuce for underliner

Serves 2

Vinaigrette Ingredients:
1/2 cup extra virgin olive oil
1/4 cup balsamic vinegar
fresh basil and garlic to taste

1. Grill or broil tuna steak. Allow to cool, then cut into large chunks.
2. Halve or quarter the potatoes and cook until just tender and chill.
3. Briefly blanch the beans. Rinse under cold water and chill.
4. Cut vegetables into large chunks or wedges.
5. Quarter the egg.
6. Arrange all elements of the dish on a large serving plate. Splash with vinaigrette and sprinkle with salt and pepper.
7. Use remaining dressing as dip.

McCormick's Fish House
Denver

Wild Mountain Mushroom Salad

Serves 2

6 tablespoons mountain mushroom variety
4 tablespoons frisee
6 tablespoons mixed greens
3 basil leaves, chiffonade
1/2 peach, sliced 1/4" thick
1/2 granny smith apple, sliced 1/4" thick
3 tablespoons grapeseed oil
salt and pepper to taste

1. Grill mark apples and peaches prior to service (optional).
2. In mixing bowl, toss greens, frisee, basil, mushrooms, and 1/2 of the peach and apple with grapeseed oil. Season with salt and pepper.
3. Garnish with the remainder of the apples and peaches.

Meritage
Broomfield

Corn Chutney

2 cups corn kernels (fresh, frozen or canned)
10 fresh tomatillos, cleaned and cut in half
2 bunches green onions, finely chopped
2 cloves garlic, chopped
1 red bell pepper, finely diced
1 medium onion, finely diced
2 Pablano chilis, finely diced
2 tablespoons butter
1/2 cup brown sugar
1/2 cup balsamic vinegar
1 tablespoon chili powder
1 teaspoon salt
1 teaspoon black pepper
1 teaspoon oregano leaf

Makes 2 Quarts

1. In a sauce pan, melt butter and brown sugar and mix together. Add all vegetables and seasoning. Mix and cook thoroughly. Stirring continuously. Add balsamic vinegar and continue to cook and stir.
2. Pour into jars or serve warm with fish or chicken. Also goes well with chips or tortillas.

Ski Tip Lodge
Keystone

Apple Apricot Salad

Serves 4 - 6

2 medium Granny Smith apples
2 medium Red Delicious apples
1 cup grapes (red and green)
2 cups peach slices, drained
1 cup pineapple chunks, drained
1 package (3.5 ounce) vanilla pudding, instant dry mix
2/3 cups apricot nectar juice

1. In a large bowl, whisk together apricot juice and pudding mix.
2. Cut peach slices in bite-size pieces. Wash fresh fruit. Core apples and cut in bite-size pieces.
3. Add peaches, pineapple, apples, and grapes to apricot mixture, stir gently to coat.
4. Chill before serving.

Baldpate Inn
Estes Park

Anaheim Chicken Salad

1 1/2 pounds cooked chicken meat
3/4 cup mayonnaise
2 tablespoons dijon mustard
1/2 large, ripe tomato, diced
1/4 cup roasted anaheim chilis, diced
2 tablespoons cilantro, chopped
1/2 cup black beans, cooked
2 tablespoons lime juice
1 teaspoon salt
1/2 teaspoon pepper

Serves 4

1. Shred the chicken meat.
2. Place all ingredients, excluding salt and pepper, into a mixing bowl. Stir together with large spoon.
3. Add seasoning and stir again.
4. Cover and refrigerate.
5. Serve on bread as a sandwich, over salad with your favorite vinaigrette or serve as is.

Table Mountain Inn
Golden

Colorado Pine Nut Salad

Serves 6

1/4 cup pine nuts
2 cloves garlic, peeled
1 cup water
1/4 teaspoon salt
1 teaspoon dijon mustard
2 tablespoons white wine vinegar
1/2 cup virgin olive oil
1 large head romaine lettuce, torn into pieces
freshly ground black pepper to taste
1/4 cup coarsely shredded Parmesan cheese

1. Toast pine nuts under the broiler until golden brown and set aside.
2. In a small saucepan, boil the garlic in water for 10 minutes and drain.
3. In a large salad bowl, mash the garlic and salt to a paste. Whisk in mustard and vinegar. Add oil in a stream, whisking the dressing until the oil is emulsified.
4. Add romaine lettuce to dressing, toss well and season with pepper. Sprinkle Parmesan cheese and pine nuts over salad and serve.

North Fork Guest Ranch
Shawnee

Colorado Cole Slaw

Cole Slaw Ingredients:
4 cups shredded cabbage (mix 50% Red and 50% Napa)
3/4 cup Citronette dressing
2 tablespoons fresh cilantro, chopped
1 avocado
2 fresh ripe tomatoes
1 jicama
salt and pepper to taste

Serves 4

Citronette Dressing Ingredients:
1/8 cup garlic, chopped
1/2 cup fresh lime juice
1/4 cup fresh lemon juice
1/2 cup creamy dijon mustard
1/2 tablespoon Kosher salt
1/4 tablespoon black pepper

1. To prepare citronette, combine all of the non-oil ingredients in a large mixing bowl. Add oil in a slow and steady stream while whipping rapidly until dressing is thick and emulsified.
2. Toss shredded cabbage in a large bowl with Citronette and cilantro until cabbage is well coated.
3. Place 1 cup of the tossed cabbage in the center of each of four plates.
4. Slice the tomatoes, avocados and skinned jicama thinly and fan out on each plate in 3 fans, equally spaced around the plate.

SNOWMASS CLUB

Sage Restaurant
Snowmass Village

Salad of Arugula, Country Ham, & Aged Goats' Cheese Vinaigrette

Serves 4

4 shallots, peeled and julienned
1/4 cup rice wine vinegar
1/4 cup white wine
1/2 cup oil
salt and pepper to taste
1/2 cup crumbled aged goats' cheese
1 pound arugula, washed, dried, and picked
1/2 cup country ham, julienned

1. In a small saucepan over high heat, combine shallots, vinegar and wine. Reduce by half, then cool to room temperature.
2. Whisk oil into shallot mixture and season with salt and pepper. Fold in goats' cheese.
3. In a large bowl, combine half of the goats' cheese vinaigrette, arugula and country ham, tossing gently.
4. Divide salad between 4 chilled plates. Drizzle with extra vinaigrette.

Alice's Restaurant
Ward

Seared Ahi & Lump Crab Salad with Lemon Arugula & Black Sesame Vinaigrette

2 ounces Ahi, sliced and slightly pounded

Lump Crab Ingredients:
1/2 pound jumbo lump crab meat
4 cups mayonnaise
4 tablespoons fresh herbs, chopped
1/2 cup green onion wings
cayenne and Old Bay Spices

Serves
4

Black Sesame Vinaigrette Ingredients:
1 quart olive oil or canola oil
1/3 cup sesame oil
1 1/4 cups rice wine vinegar
1/4 cup black and white sesame seeds
1/4 tablespoon ginger, minced
1/3 bunch cilantro, chopped semi fine
1/4 tablespoon ginger powder
1/4 cup sugar
1/4 tablespoon salt

1. Prepare Black Sesame Vinaigrette. Pour vinegar in large mixing bowl. Slowly whisk in oils. Add ginger, seeds and cilantro. Adjust seasoning as needed.
2. Combine all lump crab ingredients. Season to taste with salt, cayenne and Old Bay.
3. Place Ahi slice on cutting board, roll in crab meat mixture like a tootsie roll.
4. Sear Ahi lightly and fast on all sides. Cut on the bias.
5. In mixing bowl toss mixed greens with vinaigrette and season with salt and pepper.

Meritage
Broomfield

Butternut Squash Bisque with Lobster

1 1/2 quarts lobster stock (can be purchased in specialty food stores or direct mail catalogues)
3 3/4 pounds butternut squash
1 1/8 pints heavy cream
salt and pepper to taste

Serves 6

1. Cut butternut squash in half lengthwise and place with the cut side down on a greased sheet pan.
2. Roast squash at 350 degrees for approximately 1 hour.
3. Scrape squash meat from the skin and puree in a food processor.
4. Mix squash with heavy cream, then add the lobster stock.
5. Simmer until "bisque" consistency is achieved.

Lobster stock can be substituted with lobster base and water. Lobster meat chunks can be added to the soup just before serving.

Ludwig's
Vail

Country Style Roasted Corn Chowder

1 quart chicken stock
1/3 quart heavy cream
1/3 pint kernel corn
2/3 cup yellow onions, diced
1/3 cup carrots, diced
1/3 cup celery, diced
1/3 cup raw bacon, diced
3 tablespoons red bell pepper, diced
3 tablespoons green bell pepper, diced
2/3 cup potatoes, diced
2 teaspoons fresh thyme, chopped
2 teaspoons garlic, chopped
1 teaspoon salt
1/3 tablespoon white pepper
5 tablespoons butter
5 tablespoons flour

Serves 4 - 6

1. In a heavy sauce pan render fat from bacon. When fat is rendered, add onions, celery and carrots. Sweat for 15 - 20 minutes, or until vegetables are done. Add garlic and thyme and sweat for another 2 minutes.
2. Combine chicken stock, cream and potatoes and bring to a boil.
3. While stock and cream are heating, roast corn in the oven at 350 degrees for 15 minutes, stirring constantly to make sure it roasts evenly.
4. In medium sauce pan add butter and melt. Add flour and mix well.
5. When stock mixture comes to a boil, add corn and peppers. Bring back to a boil. Add flour and butter mixture to stock. Stir until completely dissolved. Bring to a boil and season with salt and white pepper.

Garden Terrace
Englewood

Seafood Stew

Serves 2

4 raw shrimp
8 PEI mussels
10 clams
2 ounces salmon
2 ounces tuna
2 ounces lobster (if available)
4 cups tomato fennel broth
2 tablespoons shallots, chopped
8 basil leaves, julienned
8 tomato slices, julienned
4 tablespoons carrot, diced
2 pieces grilled bread
white wine

1. Sauté mussels, clams and shrimp. Add tuna and salmon (and lobster if available). Add shallots, carrots, basil.
2. Deglaze with white wine and add tomatoes.
3. Serve in large pasta bowl with a piece of grilled bread.

Clam Chowder

4 cups onions, diced 1/4 inch
4 cups celery, diced 1/4 inch
8 cups potatoes in water
2 1/2 pounds fresh clams in juice
1 quart heavy cream
1 quart half & half
1 1/4 quarts clam stock
2/3 teaspoon thyme
2/3 teaspoon pepper
1/3 cup bacon fat
2 tablespoons roux (equal parts butter & flour cooked together)

Serves 10-20

1. Heat bacon fat.
2. Sauté onions for 3 - 5 minutes. Add celery for 3 minutes. Add potatoes and water, clam juice, stock, thyme and pepper and boil for 5 minutes. Add half and half and cream. Add clams and roux and simmer for 15 - 20 minutes.

Friar Tuck's Restaurant
Thornton

Red Pepper Soup

Serves 12

1 yellow onion, diced
1 tablespoon garlic cloves
1/2 can roasted red peppers
2 quarts chicken stock
1/2 bunch basil leaves
1/2 quart heavy cream
salt and pepper to taste
corn starch as needed
goat cheese for garnish
pesto sauce for garnish

1. Sweat onions and garlic. Add remaining ingredients and simmer for 30 minutes.
2. Puree well after cooking.
3. Season and thicken with corn starch.
4. Garnish with goat cheese and pesto and serve.

Tuscany
Denver

Grilled Lime Chicken Gazpacho

Serves 6

6 skinless chicken breasts
(1) #10 can plum tomatoes
1 cup celery, sliced
1 cup cucumbers, sliced and ground
1 1/2 cups carrots, peeled and sliced
1 1/2 cups green bell peppers, cored and chopped
1 1/3 cups red bell peppers, cored and chopped
3/4 cup onions, sliced
3/4 can V-8 juice
3/4 bunch parsley, rough chopped
1 teaspoon dry oregano
1 1/2 tablespoons salt
1 teaspoon black peppercorns
2 teaspoons sherry vinegar
1/2 cup olive oil

Chicken Marinade Ingredients:
1/2 cup olive oil
1/2 cup lime juice
1/4 cup parsley, oregano and cilantro, chopped (optional)

1. Grind all vegetables through fine grinder attachment in grinder or processor.
2. Mix all ingredients and allow to sit overnight.
3. Preservice, stir in 2 teaspoons sherry vinegar to 2 quarts of soup. Also whisk in 1/2 cup of olive oil to same ratio above. Check seasoning.
4. Marinate chicken in lime juice, chopped herbs and olive oil for 3 hours. Grill just before serving.
5. Serve chicken breast in Gazpacho.

Meritage
Broomfield

Black Bean Soup

Serves 12

1 large celery stalk, diced
1 carrot, diced
1 small onion, diced
1 leek (white part only), diced
2 garlic cloves, minced
1 ounce vegetable oil
1 teaspoon thyme
1 teaspoon ground cumin
1/2 teaspoon cayenne pepper
1/2 teaspoon white pepper
1 bay leaf
2 ounces Canadian Bacon, diced
1 ounce tomato paste
1 cup black beans, dried
6 cups chicken stock (or canned broth)

1. Cook vegetables, garlic and vegetable oil in large sauce pan for 5 minutes until onions are translucent.
2. Add spices, tomato paste and Canadian Bacon and cook for 5 minutes, (stirring continuously).
3. Add black beans and chicken stock and simmer for 2 1/2 to 3 hours until beans are tender.
4. After soup has cooled, place it in a blender and "pulse" it a couple of times. The consistency should remain chunky.
5. Adjust seasoning to taste.

SNOWMASS CLUB™

Sage Restaurant
Snowmass Village

Steak Soup

1 pound beef sirloin
1 onion, diced medium
1 large carrot, diced medium
2/3 cup celery, diced medium
1 potato, diced medium
3/4 quart beef broth
3/4 quart V-8 Juice
2/3 cup chopped canned tomatoes
3/4 quart water
black pepper
garlic salt
12 sour dough rolls

Serves 12

1. Cut beef into 1" thick steaks and rub with black pepper and garlic salt. Broil to about medium. Trim off all fat.
2. Cut broiled steak into 3/4" cubes.
3. Sauté onions and celery in pot until transparent. Add steak, vegetables, beef broth and V-8. Heat until boiling. Add water and boil 20 minutes. Reduce heat and simmer for 2 hours.
4. To serve, cut top off of roll and scoop out center to make a bowl. Pour soup into bread bowl and let it run over sides.

Garden Terrace
Colorado Springs

Sweet Potato Bisque

Serves 5

3 yams, peeled
1 1/2 cloves garlic
1/2 onion, diced
3/4 carrot, peeled
1 1/4 teaspoons basil
1 1/2 teaspoons thyme
5/8 bay leaf
3 1/4 tablespoons brown sugar
1 5/8 tablespoons brandy
7/8 teaspoon cinnamon
1 5/8 pints chicken stock
1 5/8 cups cream
salt and pepper to taste

1. Bring all ingredients, excluding cream, salt and pepper to a boil and reduce to a simmer.
2. Cook for 1 1/2 hours then remove from heat.
3. Puree in food processor while adding cream, salt and pepper.

Centennial Restaurant
Denver

Strawberry Soup

1 pint strawberries
1 / 2 cup Riesling wine
2 tablespoons honey
1 cinnamon stick
1 / 4 cup sugar
3 tablespoons water
optional: Creme de Menthe to taste

Serves 2

Garnish:
1 sliced strawberry
1 / 4 ounce mint, chopped
plain yogurt (for design)

1. Make a syrup of 1 / 4 cup water, 3 tablespoons water and cinnamon stick. Cook down to the consistency of a simple syrup.
2. To syrup add cleaned, quartered strawberries and wine. Bring to a boil. Add honey and creme de menthe.
3. Refrigerate until chilled. Garnish and serve.

The Tavern
Colorado Springs

The Swan's Wild Mushroom Soup

Serves 6 - 8

2 tablespoons dried Porcini mushrooms
3 cloves garlic, chopped
1/2 cup Shiitake mushrooms, sliced (or other wild mushroom)
1 cup white wine
1/2 cup dry sack sherry
2 cups heavy cream
1 tablespoon sea salt or kosher salt
1 tablespoon white pepper
1/2 cup Gruyere cheese, grated
1/4 bulb fennel, diced
1/4 root celriac, diced
1/2 pound butter
1/2 cup flour
1 cup water
salt and pepper to taste

1. Soak dried Porcini mushrooms over night in a cup of water, reserving the mushroom flavored water for the soup.
2. Heat the butter in a large sauce pan until it foams and add the diced fennel, onion, garlic and celriac. Stir over medium heat being careful not to brown the vegetables.
3. Add the sliced fresh shitake mushrooms, then gently stir in the flour.
4. Now add the white wine, sherry and Porcini mushrooms, including the soaking liquid. Bring this to a simmer then stir in the heavy cream. Bring back to a simmer and gently whisk in the Gruyere cheese.
5. Add salt and pepper to taste.
6. Garnish with chopped olives.

The Swan
Englewood

Tomato Chowder

3/4 cup carrots, diced
3/4 cup celery, diced
3/4 cup onion, diced
3/4 cup peeled potatoes, diced
1/4 tablespoon garlic, minced
1/8 tablespoon dry thyme
1 cup fresh tomatoes, diced
2 teaspoons olive oil
2 cups tomato juice
4 cups chicken stock
1/4 bay leaves
salt and pepper to taste

Serves 10

1. Sauté carrots, celery, onions and potatoes in olive oil with garlic and thyme. Add tomatoes and tomato juice and cook for 15 minutes. Add chicken stock and bay leaves and cook for additional 45 minutes.
2. Thicken soup with roux* and season to taste.

*Roux is equal parts of butter and flour. Cook roux for 5 minutes then slowly add to hot soup by mixing with a wire whisk.

C Lazy U Ranch
Granby

Pesce's Clam Chowder

Serves 12

1/2 pound butter
1 large yellow onion, diced
1/2 bunch celery, diced
4 cloves garlic, minced
3/4 cup dry white wine
1 1/2 cups all-purpose flour
1 quart heavy cream
1 1/2 quarts milk
1 1/2 tablespoons Worcestershire sauce
2 tablespoons Tabasco sauce
2 teaspoons dry parsley
1 teaspoon rubbed sage
1 teaspoon thyme leaf
1 teaspoon salt
1 teaspoon ground black pepper
3 pounds fresh chopped clams in juice
2 1/2 pounds cooked red skin potatoes, diced

1. In a heavy bottom, 3 gallon stock pot over medium-high heat, cook onion, celery, and garlic until translucent. Add white wine and reduce by 2/3.
2. Remove from heat and stir in flour until absorbed and forms a paste.
3. Cook mixture over medium heat for 3 minutes, stirring continuously. Gradually add cream and milk while stirring to avoid lumps and to keep from burning.
4. Add seasonings and bring up to simmer. Add clams with juice and potatoes. Return to simmer and serve.

COPPER MOUNTAIN RESORT

Pesce Fresco
Copper Mountain

Tomato-Cheddar Soup

2 cups onion, chopped
2 cups celery stalks, chopped
5 cups stewed tomatoes
2 2/3 cups heavy cream
3 1/4 cups water
1/8 box corn starch
1 1/8 teaspoons garlic, minced
2 teaspoons Italian herbs
1 1/8 teaspoons salt
5/8 teaspoons white pepper
1 1/8 teaspoon cajun seasoning
5/8 teaspoon sugar
2 1/8 tablespoon olive oil
Cheddar cheese to taste

Serves 8

1. Sauté onions and celery in olive oil. Add tomatoes, water and seasonings. Simmer for about 30 minutes and thicken with corn starch.
2. Divide among 8 bowls and top with generous amount of grated Cheddar cheese.

Bully Ranch
Vail

Cream of Tomato Soup

Serves 6

(2) 14 1/2 ounce cans diced tomatoes
1 1/2 teaspoons onion powder
1 teaspoon celery salt
1 pint chicken stock
1 1/2 teaspoons dried basil
1/4 teaspoon black pepper
salt to taste
1 cup whipping cream
2 tablespoons butter

1. In a large pot, combine tomato, onion powder, celery salt and chicken stock. Bring to a boil. Reduce heat and simmer for 30 minutes.
2. Add basil, pepper and salt. Simmer an additional 10 minutes. Stir in cream and butter.
3. Serve warm.

Waunita Hot Springs
Gunnison

Mango Melon Soup

1 small melon, peeled and cubed
1 ripe banana
1 mango, peeled and cubed
1 tablespoon lemon juice
1 tablespoon honey
dash vanilla
6 mint leaves for garnish
6 raspberries for garnish

Serves 6

1. Place melon cubes in blender and process until smooth.
2. Add banana, 1/4 cup mango cubes, lemon juice, honey and vanilla and blend until smooth.
3. Chill mixture for several hours or overnight. Chill remaining mango cubes separately.
4. To serve, divide mango cubes among six parfait cups. Stir chilled mixture and pour equally over the fruit. Garnish with raspberries and mint leaves.

Two Sisters Inn
a bed and breakfast

Two Sisters Inn - a bed & breakfast
Manitou Springs

Cantaloupe Gazpacho

Serves 6

2 cantaloupes, peeled and chopped
1/2 yellow bell pepper, chopped
1/2 leek, white only, chopped
2 cucumbers, peeled, chopped
1 carrot, peeled, chopped
1 stalk celery, chopped
5 golden tomatoes, quartered
1/3 bunch cilantro, chopped
1/4 cup rice wine vinegar
1/2 lime, juice of
1/2 orange, juice of

1. Combine all ingredients, excluding cilantro, in a blender or food processor and mix until smooth.
2. Strain. Add cilantro. Add salt and white pepper to taste.

Golden Gazpacho

2 1/2 pounds hydroponic or greenhouse yellow tomatoes
4 yellow bell peppers
4 yellow squash
2 jalapenos
2 quarts water
1 cup olive oil
1/2 cup red wine vinegar
salt and pepper
fresh cilantro for garnish
12 grilled shrimp for garnish

Serves 12

1. Combine all ingredients, excluding garnish items, in a food processor and puree.
2. Serve in soup bowl with cilantro and shrimp garnish.

Bully Ranch BBQ Sauce

Serves 8

2 1/8 cups chili sauce
2 1/8 cups ketchup
1/4 cup onion, minced
1 tablespoon garlic, minced
1/4 pound bacon, minced
1 1/4 cups orange juice
5/8 cup red wine
2 teaspoons chili powder, hot
2 teaspoons paprika
1/2 teaspoon white pepper
2 1/2 tablespoons red wine vinegar
1 1/4 tablespoons molasses
1 1/4 tablespoons Worcestershire sauce

1. Place all ingredients in a large pot over medium heat and let simmer for 1 hour. Let cool.
2. Store in airtight container. (Keeps in refrigerator for 1 month and can be frozen)

Bully Ranch
Vail

Pastas & Vegetables

Thai Pasta Sauce

2 1/2 cups oyster sauce
1 1/2 cups hoisin sauce
1/4 cup sesame oil (blended, not pure)
1/4 teaspoon cayenne
1/2 cup rice wine vinegar
3 tablespoons pickled ginger
2 tablespoons fresh garlic, chopped
1 to 2 cups water as needed

Serves 20

1. Combine all ingredients in blender or food processor and blend well. Add water as needed to achieve consistency of pancake syrup.
2. Serve over Thai noodles.

Palm Court
Glenwood Springs

Shrimp and Scallop Thai Pasta

Serves 2

6 shrimp
2 scallops
4 tablespoons olive oil
2 teaspoon garlic, chopped
2 teaspoon shallots, chopped
5 snowpeas
1 tablespoon carrots, shredded
1 tablespoon bean sprouts
1 tablespoon cashews, chopped
6 tablespoons bean thread noodles
1/2 fresh Thai chili, chopped
1/4 cup rice wine vinegar
1/2 cup white wine
1 teaspoon fresh ginger, chopped
1 teaspoons mint, chopped

1. Soak the bean thread noodles in warm water for 30 minutes or until soft.
2. Sauté shrimp and scallops in olive oil for 2 minutes. Add garlic, shallots, Thai chilies, ginger and shredded carrots and cook for an additional 2 minutes on medium heat.
3. Deglaze the pan with rice wine, vinegar and white wine, let reduce by 1/3, then add snow peas and bean sprouts.
4. Let sauce reduce until vegetables are al dente. Add the mint and toss with the bean thread noodles and cashews. Adjust seasoning with salt and pepper.

The Brother's Grille
Snowmass Village

1 Grilled Vegetable Panini

10" round focaccia or baguette bread
1 cup baby field greens
4 tablespoons herbed garlic vinaigrette
1/2 cup roasted peppers
6 roma tomatoes, sliced
1/4 cup toasted pine nuts
1/2 cup marinated onions (salt, pepper, balsamic vinegar)
(6) 3/4 ounce slices Fontana cheese
1/2 cup goat cheese crumbles
1/2 cup assorted grilled vegetables (eggplant, zucchini)
2 tablespoons pesto olive oil
salt and pepper to taste

Serves 2

1. Slice bread in half lengthwise.
2. Toss field greens with herbed vinaigrette and place on bread.
3. Arrange remaining vegetables, cheeses and toasted pine nuts atop greens.
4. Drizzle with pesto olive oil and season with salt and pepper.

Compari's Restaurant
Denver

Baked Penne with Turkey Cilantro Sausage

Serves 9

Penne and Sausage Ingredients:
1 pound penne pasta
1 1/2 pounds turkey cilantro sausage
1/2 cup black beans, cooked
1 cup ricotta cheese
1/2 cup cheddar cheese, shredded
1/2 cup Mozzarella cheese, shredded
1 cup tomatoes, diced
1/2 cup red onion, julienned
1 tablespoon fresh garlic plus a pinch of chopped garlic
1 bunch cilantro, chopped
cracked black pepper to taste
1/2 cup olive oil
1 tablespoon whole butter
1 teaspoon each of cumin, paprika, and cayenne pepper
2 teaspoons Kosher salt

Roasted Red Pepper Sauce Ingredients:
3 red bell peppers
2 tablespoons Garlic
1/2 cup shallots
2 teaspoons Kosher salt
2 teaspoons ground black pepper
1/4 cup lemon juice
1 cup white wine
3 cups chicken stock
1/4 cup olive oil

1. Cook penne pasta al denté in water seasoned with garlic, salt and pepper. Strain pasta but do not wash.

Continued on next page

Restaurant 1876
Denver

2. Lightly toss pasta in olive oil and a pinch of chopped garlic.
3. Slice sausage 3/8" thick on the bias and sauté with red onions in olive oil over medium heat until onions are opaque and sausage is golden brown. Let cool.
4. Reserve half of the cheddar and Mozzarella.
5. In a large bowl, combine all other ingredients and gently blend together. Adjust seasoning to taste. Loosely place mixture inside of buttered 10" x 12" x 3" baking pan and top with remaining shredded cheeses. Bake at 325 degrees until top is golden and mixture is firm to the touch. Chill completely (at least 3 hours in the refrigerator) and turn out of pan onto cutting surface. Use 4" cookie cutter to cut circles and remove excess. Place circles back into baking pan for re-heating before service.
6. Wash peppers and lightly coat with olive oil. Place in preheated 500 degree oven until skin turns black and blisters away from the meat of the pepper. For better flavor, roast peppers to the same point over open flame. Allow peppers to cool only to the point where they are not too hot to handle. Under running water, peel away skin and remove stem and seeds. Dice roasted peppers to 3/8" squares.
7. In olive oil, sauté diced shallots until opaque. Add garlic and peppers and continue to sauté until garlic looses its sharpness and peppers are giving off a sweet aroma. Deglaze with wine and lemon juice and reduce by half. Add chicken stock and simmer for 30 minutes.
8. Remove half the sauce and puree in blender until smooth. Combine puree with diced peppers and add salt and pepper to taste.
9. To serve, place hot pasta in center of plate and top with 3 ounces roasted pepper sauce. Garnish with sprig of fresh cilantro.

Cajun Linguine Pasta with Shrimp & Crawfish Tails

Serves 2

1/2 pound linguine pasta
4 large shrimp
1/8 pound crawfish tail meat, pre-cooked
1 1/2 tablespoons scallions, chopped
1 tablespoon tomato, seeded and diced
1 teaspoon garlic, chopped
1 1/2 tablespoons Crazy Jerry's cajun seasoning
1 tablespoon unsalted butter
3/4 cup heavy whipping cream
4 tablespoons Parmesan cheese, finely shredded

Crazy Jerry's Cajun Seasoning:
4 teaspoons paprika
1 1/2 teaspoons salt
1 teaspoon dried thyme
1 teaspoon garlic powder
1/2 teaspoon cayenne pepper
1/2 teaspoon onion powder

1. Combine cajun seasoning ingredients and mix well.
2. In a medium pot bring 3/4 gallon of water, teaspoon of salt and one tablespoon canola oil to a boil. Once water reaches boil add pasta and cook for approximately 7 minutes. Stir often so noodles will not stick together.
3. Coat shrimp in 1/2 tablespoon of cajun seasoning and cook with butter for 1 minute in a medium sauté pan. Add garlic and scallions and cook for an additional minute.
4. Add heavy cream, Parmesan cheese, and remaining cajun seasoning and cook until sauce thickens. Fold in the crawfish tail meat and tomatoes.
5. Toss with a touch of parsley, finely chopped and serve.

Grand Lake Lodge
Grand Lake

Rigatoni with Pancetta & A Warm Hazelnut Vinaigrette

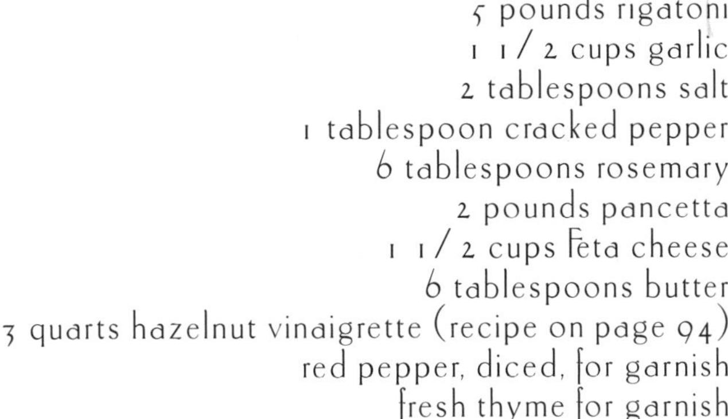

5 pounds rigatoni
1 1/2 cups garlic
2 tablespoons salt
1 tablespoon cracked pepper
6 tablespoons rosemary
2 pounds pancetta
1 1/2 cups Feta cheese
6 tablespoons butter
3 quarts hazelnut vinaigrette (recipe on page 94)
red pepper, diced, for garnish
fresh thyme for garnish

Serves 10

1. Cook rigatoni in boiling, salted water until al dente. Cool and set aside.
2. Slice pancetta into thin slices, then julienne. Reserve.
3. Pick rosemary from stem and chop very fine.
4. In sauté pan, add butter. When hot add garlic and sauté briefly. Add pancetta and sauté for 2 minutes. Add rigatoni and sauté until warm.
5. Add salt, pepper and rosemary then add vinaigrette and lower heat. Bring to simmer.
6. Remove from heat and place in bowl, crumble feta cheese over top.
9. Garnish with diced red pepper and fresh thyme.

Sunday Brunch
Englewood

Pasta Pescotore

Serves 4

3/4 cup pure olive oil
1 1/2 tablespoons fresh garlic, chopped
1 teaspoon fresh shallots, minced
12 shrimp, cleaned and deveined
12 fresh scallops
1/2 cup white wine (chardonnay)
7 large roma tomatoes, diced
1 1/2 cups leeks, chopped
1/2 cup light shrimp shell stock (or canned clam juice)
1/4 cup fresh basil
1/4 cup fresh parsley, chopped
salt and pepper to taste
1 1/2 pounds angel hair pasta, pre-cooked al dente
1/4 cup Parmesan cheese, grated

1. Pre-heat skillet over medium-high heat. Add olive oil, garlic and shallots. Cook until lightly bronzed.
2. Add shrimp and scallops and toss quickly in the pan. Deglaze with 1/4 cup of white wine.
3. Add roma tomatoes and leeks and cook for 3 - 5 minutes. Add remaining white wine, shrimp stock and fresh herbs and cook an additional 2 minutes.
4. Dip angel hair in hot water for 30 - 45 seconds. Drain well and add to skillet. Toss pasta with ingredients to marry flavors.
5. Remove from heat and serve pasta in bowls in equal portions. Artfully arrange scallops and shrimp on top of pasta and pour the remaining ingredients over the top of the dish. Sprinkle with Parmesan cheese. Serve immediately.

Henry's Italian Bistro
Durango

Mediterranean Penne Pasta

1/4 cup sundried tomatoes, diced
2 tablespoons olive oil
1 tablespoon dill weed
1 cup penne pasta
1/4 cup butter
1 medium red bell pepper, diced
1 medium gold bell pepper, diced
1 clove garlic, minced
1/4 cup flour
1 cup dry white wine
2 cups heavy cream
1/2 cup prosciutto ham, diced
1/4 cup fresh parsley, chopped
1/4 cup black olives, diced
salt to taste
freshly ground black pepper
1/4 cup Parmesan cheese, freshly grated

Serves 4

1. Soak the sundried tomatoes in olive oil with dill weed until soft (15 - 20 minutes).
2. Cook the pasta in boiling salt water until tender, but still firm. While pasta is cooking, melt butter over medium heat in a heavy sauce pan. When it is hot but not browning, add garlic and peppers and sauté until the garlic is golden. Stir in flour and let cook 1 minute. Add wine slowly, while stirring, then add cream. Simmer sauce over low heat until it bubbles and thickens (5 minutes). Stir in sundried tomatoes, ham, parsley, olives, salt and pepper to taste and heat for 3 minutes.
3. Heat a large serving bowl. Combine drained pasta and the sauce in bowl and toss gently. Sprinkle with cheese and serve immediately.

Hot Springs Restaurant
Glenwood Springs

Cajun Crevettes

Serves 1

3 medium shrimp
6 tablespoons kielbasa
6 tablespoons mushrooms
4 tablespoons cherry tomatoes
1/2 tablespoon scallions
1/2 cup heavy cream
6 tablespoons asiago cheese
1/2 cup penne pasta
2 tablespoons blended vegetable oil
1 teaspoon blackening seasoning
flour for coating

1. Coat each shrimp with flour.
2. Heat oil in a medium sauté pan over high heat. Place mushrooms in pan and sauté for 1 minute. Add shrimp and brown both sides. Add kielbasa and heavy cream. Reduce to half, then add blackening spice.
3. Remove from heat and add asiago cheese. Add cooked pasta and stir until well blended.

Estes Valley Resorts
Estes Park

Lemon-Basil Chicken with Penne Pasta

4 skinless chicken breasts
1 bunch fresh basil, chopped
2 lemons, sliced
1/2 cup olive oil
3 cloves garlic, minced
1/2 cup white wine
2 cups heavy cream
1 cup Gorgonzola cheese, crumbled
1/2 cup Parmigiana cheese, grated
3 roma tomatoes, diced
1/2 bunch asparagus, blanched
1 pound (cooked weight) penne pasta, cooked al dente

Serves 4

1. Clean chicken and cut into thin strips. Marinate in basil, lemons and 1/4 cup olive oil in refrigerator overnight.
2. Sauté chicken strips in a hot pan with the remainder of the olive oil. When chicken is almost cooked, add the garlic and cook slightly to release the flavors.
3. Add white wine and reduce liquid by 1/2. Add the cream and cheeses and reduce until a smooth thick sauce-like consistency is achieved. Add tomatoes and asparagus, mix well, then fold in the cooked hot pasta (season with salt and pepper as needed). Garnish with fresh basil tops and serve.

Bravo! Ristorante
Denver

The Swan's Creamy Mashed Potatoes with Roasted Garlic and Celriac

Serves 4

1 whole bulb garlic
1 celery root, peeled, diced large
5 russet or Colorado yukon potatoes, cut into fours
1 cup heavy cream
1/4 pound unsalted butter
pinch nutmeg
salt and pepper to taste

1. Roast garlic bulb in foil with a dash of olive oil at 350 degrees for 1 hour. While warm, squeeze garlic out of each roasted clove.
2. Place cut celery root and potatoes into a large sauce pan of cold water (about 1 1/2 quarts). Bring to boil and simmer until potatoes and celery root are soft in the center.
3. Mix cream and butter together until cream is incorporated into butter.
4. In a separate pan, bring creamed butter to a simmer and shut off, keeping warm.
5. When potatoes are cooked, drain until quite dry. While still warm, push potato/celery root mixture and roasted garlic through a food mill, heavy strainer, or potato ricer.
6. Whisk cream and butter into potato/celery root mixture, being careful not to over mix as this will change the texture of your potatoes.
7. Add salt, pepper and nutmeg to taste.
8. Keep covered until ready to serve.

The Swan
Englewood

Colorado Corn Risotto

3 tablespoons olive oil
4 tablespoons onions, diced fine
1 tablespoon garlic, chopped
1 1/4 cup Arborio rice
3/4 cup white wine
6 cups chicken or corn stock, hot
6 tablespoons corn pudding
1 cup corn kernels
2 tablespoons chives, chopped
2 tablespoons butter
1/4 cup Parmesan cheese, grated
1/4 cup chive oil
salt and pepper to taste

Serves 6

1. Heat olive oil in a medium sauce pot. Add onions and cook until translucent, then add garlic and cook for 30 seconds.
2. Add rice and stir with a wooden spoon to coat the rice with the oil. Add wine and stir until it is almost cooked out.
3. Cover the rice with corn or chicken stock and stir until the stock is absorbed. Continue covering rice with stock until all 6 cups have been absorbed. Cook until rice is almost done.
4. Add the corn kernels, Parmesan and corn pudding.
5. Finish with butter, chives, salt and pepper.
6. Place risotto on 6 plates and garnish with chive oil.

The Wildflower
Vail

Wild Mushroom Sausage with Avocado Pesto

Serves 4

Wild Mushroom Sausage Ingredients:
1 tablespoon whole butter
1/2 tablespoon garlic, chopped
1/2 tablespoon shallots, chopped
1 cup Shiitake mushrooms, stems removed and sliced
1 cup domestic mushrooms, sliced
1 cup Portobello mushrooms, sliced
1 tablespoon basil, chopped
1 whole egg
1/4 cup Parmesan, grated
1/2 cup Japanese bread crumbs
Kosher salt and black pepper to taste

Avocado Pesto Ingredients:
1 avocado
2 tablespoons cilantro, chopped
1/4 cup pine nuts, toasted
1 teaspoon garlic, chopped
2 tablespoons Parmesan, grated
1 teaspoon fresh lime juice
2 tablespoons olive oil
Kosher salt and black pepper to taste

1. To prepare avocado pesto, chop pine nuts well in food processor. Add all remaining ingredients, except oil and process until fairly smooth. Slowly add the oil in a slow and steady stream.
2. Season to taste with salt and pepper.
3. Cover pesto with plastic wrap touching the surface of the pesto to prevent browning.

Continued on next page

SNOWMASS CLUB

Sage Restaurant
Snowmass Village

4. To prepare wild mushroom sausage, melt butter in hot sauté pan. Add garlic and shallots and sauté until soft. Add sliced mushrooms and sauté until they start to become crispy. Remove from heat and cool mixture.
5. Combine half of the cooled mixture with the remaining ingredients, reserving 1/4 of the bread crumbs for the crust, in a food processor and chop well.
6. Combine the 2 mushroom mixtures together and season to taste with salt and pepper.
7. Form into 1 1/2 ounce patties and crust with the remaining bread crumbs.
8. For service, cook in a hot sauté pan, in either butter or oil, until crisp on both sides. Serve on top of a dollop of avocado pesto.

Poppy Seed Sour Cream Potatoes

Serves 5 - 6

3 large potatoes
1/2 cup sharp cheddar cheese, shredded
1/2 pint sour cream
1/4 cup half and half
1/4 cup poppy seeds
6 green onions with tops, chopped
salt and pepper to taste

1. Peel and dice potatoes. Boil until tender.
2. Combine potatoes with remaining ingredients and place in lightly greased pan.
3. Bake at 350 degrees for 20 - 25 minutes, covered, then uncover and bake an additional 20 minutes.

Latigo Ranch
Kremmling

Tavern Garden Burger

Serves 8

1/2 cup carrots, finely diced
1/2 cup green zucchini, finely diced
1/4 cup yellow onion, finely diced
1/2 cup lentils
3 cloves garlic, mashed
1/2 cup wheat bulgar
1/2 cup boiling water
3 ounces tofu, mashed
2 tablespoons flour
1/2 cup bread crumbs
3 tablespoons soy sauce
salt and pepper to taste
8 slices tomato
8 slices eggplant, 1/4" thick
8 Kaiser grain rolls or hamburger buns
8 ounces marinara sauce

1. Pre-soak the lentils in water.
2. Cook lentils until done and cool.
3. Pour boiling water over bulgar and cool.
4. Blanch carrots, squash, and onions. Strain and cool.
5. Mix all ingredients in bowl and season. Mix until it reaches a thick enough consistency to make patties.
6. Heat a non-stick skillet and spray with a vegetable coating. Sauté patties on both sides until brown and crisp.
7. Place patty on bun and garnish with grilled eggplant and tomato. Serve marinara sauce on top of burger or on the side.

Tavern
Colorado Springs

Spinach & Wild Mushroom Strudel

Serves 4 - 6

4 cups spinach leaves, cleaned and deveined
1 cup leeks, 1/4" dice
3/4 cup Shiitake mushrooms, cleaned & steamed, 1/4" slice
3/4 cup oysters, cleaned & steamed, 1/4" slice
2 tablespoons garlic, minced
1/4 cup olive oil
salt and pepper to taste
3/4 cup Boursin cheese
5 sheets phyllo dough
1/2 cup clarified butter
1 cup white bread crumbs
1/2 cup parsley and chervil, chopped

1. Heat olive oil, add garlic and leeks and cook until tender. Add mushrooms and spinach, stir with spoon until well blended. Drain any excess fluid and store in the refrigerator.
2. Lay out phyllo dough (you may want to cover with a damp towel until you are ready to use).
3. On parchment paper, place one sheet of dough and brush dough with butter mixture lightly with pastry brush, beginning with the corners of the dough.
4. Sprinkle the sheet of dough with bread crumbs and herb mix. Repeat steps 3 and 4 with five layers of dough.
5. Place filling about 2" from the bottom and make channel in the spinach to place the Boursin cheese. Using the parchment paper, roll the strudel tightly. Brush rolled strudel with butter and score with a serrated knife where you would like to cut the strudel when it is done.
6. Bake at 400 degrees for 10 - 12 minutes. Serve.

Allie's American Grille
Denver

Risotto with Wild Mushrooms

2 cups Arborio rice
4 tablespoons butter
1 cup white wine
3 cups chicken stock
1/4 cup onion, diced
2 ounces dry wild mushrooms, soaked & chopped rough
1/2 teaspoon garlic
1/2 cup demi glace
1/2 cup cream
parsley for garnish, chopped
salt and pepper to taste

Serves 4

1. Sweat the onions in clarified butter and add rice. Add just enough wine to almost cover the rice and stir until the liquid is absorbed. Add stock to cover rice and stir until liquid is absorbed. Repeat process until all stock is absorbed. Check to see if rice is cooked and add more stock if needed.
2. Sauté the mushrooms and garlic. Add the cooked rice.
3. Moisten with demi glace and add the cream.
4. Garnish with chopped parsley and serve.

Spencer's
Breckenridge

Seafood Entrees

Grilled Salmon Roulade with Aioli

3 - 8 ounces salmon filets
1/4 cup fresh basil, chopped
1 teaspoon salt
1 teaspoon pepper
1/2 cup mayonnaise
1 tablespoon garlic, chopped
2 teaspoons lemon juice
1 teaspoon shallots, chopped
1/4 cup olive oil

Serves 3

1. Make a cut lengthwise beginning on one end of each salmon filet, 1/3 the thickness of the filet and proceed to cut the opposite end, stopping 1/4" from the end. Repeat on the 2/3 remaining. Open the filet out and it should be 3 times as long.
2. Sprinkle the chopped basil on the salmon and roll the salmon into a roulade using a toothpick to hold together.
3. Make aioli by mixing mayonnaise, garlic, shallots, lemon juice and season with salt and pepper. Set aside.
4. Pre-heat charcoal grill.
5. Coat salmon with olive oil and grill to desired temperature.
6. Serve with aioli on top.

The Brother's Grille
Snowmass Village

Braised Lobster Medallions & Sea Scallops Roasted Red Pepper Sabayon

Serves 6

Roasted Red Pepper Sabayon Ingredients:
1 tablespoon olive oil
2 red bell peppers
1/2 cup chicken stock, hot
1 teaspoon garlic, minced
2 egg yolks
2 tablespoons white wine
1/2 cup clarified butter
pinch cayenne pepper

Yellow Pepper & Basil Risotto Ingredients:
2 yellow bell peppers, seeded and chopped
1 teaspoon garlic, minced
1 teaspoon shallots, minced
1.4 cup extra virgin olive oil
1 cup white wine
3 cups chicken stock
1 1/2 cups Arborio rice
2 tablespoons fresh basil leaves, julienned
3 tablespoons butter

Braised Lobster Medallions and Sea Scallops Ingredients:
6 Maine lobster tails, par boiled
12 jumbo sea scallops, patted dry
2 cups spinach, stemmed and cleaned
1/4 cup olive oil
10 tablespoons white wine
1 tablespoon garlic, minced
1 tablespoon shallots, minced
1 lemon, juice of
1/2 cup butter
1/4 red, yellow, green peppers, fine dice
salt and pepper to taste

Continued on next page

Palace Arms
Denver

1. Prepare Roasted Red Pepper Sabayon by first rubbing peppers with oil then roasting at 400 degrees until skin blisters. Remove peppers from oven, place in bowl, cover with plastic wrap and let cool. When cool, peel skin, remove seeds and chop.
2. In food processor, puree peppers with hot chicken stock and keep warm.
3. In stainless steel bowl combine garlic, egg yolks, white wine and cayenne pepper. Place bowl over pot of simmering water. With a wire whisk, continually stir until eggs begin to cook and mixture begins to thicken. Remove from heat and slowly whisk in clarified butter. Add the pepper puree, mix, adjust seasoning and keep warm.
4. Next prepare the Yellow Pepper and Basil Risotto. In a medium, thick bottom sauce pot heat 2 tablespoons of olive oil and sauté peppers, garlic and shallots until tender. Add 1/2 of the wine and 1/2 of the stock and simmer until peppers are soft.
5. Puree in food processor and keep warm.
6. In sauce pot add remaining olive oil and rice and stir until rice is warm and coated with oil. Add remaining wine, stock and pepper puree. Simmer rice, stirring occasionally until rice is soft. Add basil leaves, adjust seasoning, remove from stove and keep warm.
7. Now it is time to prepare the Lobster and Shallots. Add 2 tablespoons of olive oil to pan and sear scallops on one side until lightly browned. Turn scallops and add lobster, 1/2 of garlic, 1/2 of shallots, white wine, 1/2 of lemon juice and butter. Simmer on stove until scallops are done and lobster is hot. Remove pan from stove and keep warm.
8. In a separate, pre-heated sauté pan add remaining olive oil, shallots, garlic, spinach and lemon juice and sauté until spinach wilts. Season with salt and pepper and remove pan from stove.
9. Assemble on plates and serve.

Jumbo Lump Crab Cakes with Tangerine Vinaigrette

Serves 6

Crab Cake Ingredients:
3 pounds shrimp, peeled and deveined
5 bunches green onions, sliced on bias
3 pounds jumbo lump crab meat
1 1/2 quarts heavy cream
5 eggs
1/3 cup French's mustard
1 1/4 teaspoon Worcestershire sauce
2 teaspoons Tabasco sauce
1 tablespoon garlic puree
Japanese bread crumbs

Tangerine Vinaigrette Ingredients:
1/2 cup shallots, shredded or diced
2 tablespoons sugar
3 cups orange juice, reduced to 2 cups
4 cups canola oil
1 cup oil
salt and pepper to taste

1. Sauté green onions and garlic slowly; cool.
2. To make mousse first, puree shrimp, add seasonings, blend scrap and slowly add cream while turning. Place in mixing bowl in a bowl of ice.
3. Fold crab and green onions into mousse. Mix in bread crumbs a small amount at a time to help with binding. Portion into pathes and toss in bread crumbs to coat.
4. Sear Crab Cakes.
5. Toss greens with vinaigrette. Place Crab Cake on greens and ladle vinaigrette around plate.

OMNI INTERLOCKEN RESORT

Meritage
Broomfield

BBQ Salmon with Japanese Vinaigrette

1 cup peanut oil
2 teaspoons rice vinegar
2 teaspoons sesame oil
1 tablespoons soy sauce
2 tablespoons lemon juice
2 tablespoons lime juice
pinch garlic
1/2 teaspoon brown sugar
1/2 teaspoon horseradish
pinch wasabi
(4) 8 ounce salmon filets
4 cups bok choy, chopped rough

Serves 4

1. Mix all ingredients, excluding salmon and bok choy, place in food processor and blend. Strain through a fine sieve.
2. Grill or BBQ salmon filets.
3. Serve with steamed bok choy and vinaigrette.

Spencer's
Breckenridge

Diver Scallops with Udon Noodles

Serves 4

4 tablespoons shiitake mushrooms, sliced
1 tablespoon wakame seaweed, soaked in water
5 cups hot vegetable broth
1 tablespoon miso paste
1 1/2 cups udon noodles, cooked
1/2 cup firm tofu, cut into cubes
1 green onion, finely sliced
1 fresh Kafir lime leaf
12 large sea scallops
2 tablespoons light soy sauce
fresh coriander leaves

1. Clean scallops and reserve.
2. Put the vegetable stock and miso paste in a large sauce pan and bring to a boil. Add the noodles and return to a boil. Add the seaweed, tofu, sea scallops, shiitakes and lime leaf. (Crush lime leaf in your hand prior to adding, as this will release its flavor.) Cover and simmer gently for 5 minutes. Remove lime leaf, stir in soy sauce and garnish with green onion and fresh coriander leaves.
3. Serve immediately.

Sundance Restaurant
Telluride

Grilled Tournedos of Swordfish with Fresh Herb Salade & Mousseline Potatoes

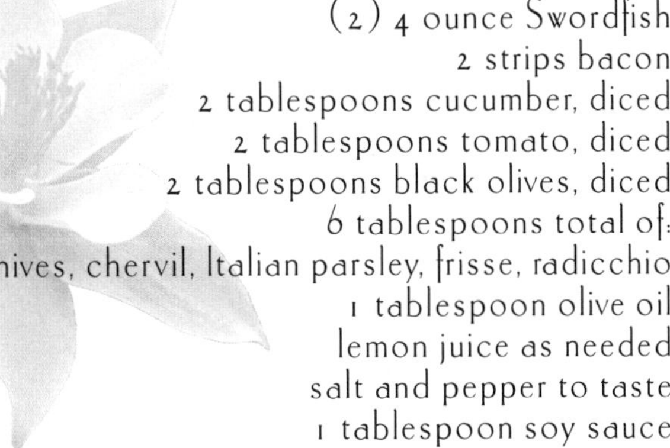

(2) 4 ounce Swordfish
2 strips bacon
2 tablespoons cucumber, diced
2 tablespoons tomato, diced
2 tablespoons black olives, diced
6 tablespoons total of:
chives, chervil, Italian parsley, frisse, radicchio
1 tablespoon olive oil
lemon juice as needed
salt and pepper to taste
1 tablespoon soy sauce

Serves 2

Mousseline Potato Ingredients:
2 medium potatoes
1-2 tablespoons butter

1. Prepare Fresh Herb Salade Sauce. Mix soy sauce, olive oil, lemon juice and black pepper. Combine with cucumber, tomatoes and black olives.
2. Wrap bacon around swordfish filet. Place Fresh Herb Salade Sauce on top and grill.
3. Prepare Mousseline Potatoes. Peel and dice potatoes, cover with water and boil until soft. Mash with butter until creamy. Salt and pepper to taste.
5. Arrange all on plate and serve.

Penrose Room
Colorado Springs

Shellfish Paella

Serves 4

1/4 cup Spanish extra virgin olive oil
1/4 cup onion, minced
1 1/2 cups short-grain rice
1 1/2 cups tomatoes, finely chopped
(4) 8 ounce bottles clam juice, heated to simmer & divided
2 bay leaves
1 teaspoon saffron threads
1 teaspoon Spanish paprika
1 teaspoon salt
3/4 teaspoon pepper, freshly ground
3 medium lobster tails
16 mussels, cleaned
16 manila clams or cockles, cleaned
16 large shrimp, shelled & deveined, with tails left on
1/2 cup peas, fresh or frozen and thawed
2 tablespoons red bell pepper strips

1. In a large, deep skillet with a tight fitting lid, heat olive oil. When hot, add onion. Cook over medium heat, stirring frequently, until onion is translucent (about 3 minutes). Stir in rice and tomatoes. Cook, stirring frequently, until rice is golden (about 5 minutes). Stir in 3 1/2 cups hot clam juice, bay leaves, saffron, paprika, salt, and pepper. Cover and simmer gently until rice is barely tender (about 10 minutes).
2. Meanwhile, remove thin shell from underside of each lobster tail (kitchen scissors work best for this); cut tails into halves lengthwise. Place tails, shell side down, in the center of the rice mixture. Cover and simmer for 5 minutes. Arrange mussels and clams around edge of pan; cover and simmer for 5 minutes. Turn lobster tails over, shell side up. Arrange shrimp around lobster.

Continued on next page

Al Mar, Inc. - Allied Member
Littleton

Gently press seafoods down into the rice mixture so that they absorb some of the liquid. Cover and simmer until shrimp are pink and firm (about 5 minutes). Add remaining 1/2 cup hot clam juice. Sprinkle with peas and red bell peppers.

3. Cover and remove from heat. Let stand for 10 - 15 minutes before serving. Discard any unopened mussels or clams. Garnish with a fresh bay leaf or coarsely chopped, flat leaf parsley.

Sole Parmesan

Serves 2

- 1/2 cup flour
- 1 egg, beaten with 1 tablespoon milk
- 6 - 8 ounces fresh Parmesan, shredded
- 1 cup flaked, dried bread crumbs
- 12 - 16 ounces boneless filet of sole (preferably petrale)
- 3 tablespoons oil for frying
- 2 tablespoons butter
- 2 tablespoons lemon juice
- 6 lemon segments, chopped
- 2 teaspoons capers
- 1 teaspoon shallots, chopped
- 1 tablespoon parsley, chopped

1. Place the flour, egg and shredded Parmesan mixed with the bread crumbs in 3 separate baking dishes. (The Parmesan must be freshly shredded, into thin pieces similar to 1/2" long toothpicks, not grated into granules or a powder.)
2. Dip filets in flour, shaking off excess, then into egg and finally into cheese mixture, taking great care to coat the fish evenly and completely.
3. Heat oil in a large non-stick sauté pan or on a range top griddle over high heat. Place fish in pan and allow to brown for 1 minute. Turn fish, taking care not to disturb the crispy browned cheese. (If coating flakes off the fish in spots, retrieve the specks of cheese and scatter them back on top of the fish.) After turning, the fish will take only 1 more minute. Remove to dinner plates.
4. Wipe oil from pan and return it to the stove or, if using the griddle, heat a sauté pan. Add remaining ingredients and cook over medium heat until the butter is slightly browned. Pour over fish.

THE OXFORD HOTEL

McCormick's Fish House
Denver

Rainbow Trout Almondine

1 trout filet, butterflied
2 tablespoons toasted almonds, sliced
4 tablespoons Amaretto liqueur
2 tablespoons butter
2 tablespoons vegetable oil
parsley, chopped for garnish

Serves
1

1. In a medium sauté pan, heat oil over high heat. Place butterflied trout into oil and sauté for 3 minutes each side. Add almonds, Amaretto and butter. Turn off heat and swirl in pan until thickened.
2. Place fish on plate, garnish with chopped parsley and serve.

EVR
Estes Valley Resorts

Aspen Lodge Restaurant
Estes Park

Warm Gold Potato Ragout with French Beans, Wild Mushrooms & Smoked CoHo Salmon

Serves 4

4 Yukon Gold Potatoes, cleaned and boiled until tender, skin on
1 cup Morel mushrooms, cleaned, trimmed and sliced
1 cup Shiitake mushrooms, cleaned, trimmed and sliced
1 cup Portobello mushrooms, cleaned, trimmed and sliced
2 cups French green beans, cleaned and blanched
3 tablespoons chervil, chopped (reserve a few sprigs)
3 tablespoons Italian parsley, chopped (reserve a few sprigs)
4 cups frisee
(4) 6 ounce portions CoHo salmon, cold smoked, skinless and boneless
olive oil
salt and pepper to taste

Ancho Honey Vinaigrette Ingredients:
4 tablespoons Ancho Chili puree
1 cup honey
1 cup white wine vinegar
2 cups peanut oil
2 tablespoons lime juice
1 / 2 bunch cilantro
1 teaspoon garlic, finely minced
4 tablespoons balsamic vinegar

1. Prepare Ancho Honey Vinaigrette. Place ancho puree, minced garlic, 1 / 2 cup honey and 1 / 2 cup white wine vinegar in blender cup, on low speed add the peanut oil in a slow steady stream to form an emulsion. Add the remaining honey and continue to adjust the consistency with the addition of the remaining white wine vinegar. Finish with balsamic vinegar and add the cilantro and puree a few seconds more. Adjust seasoning with salt and freshly ground pepper.

Continued on next page

Century Room
Aspen

2. Prepare potatoes and french beans. Sauté mushrooms in a little olive oil over high heat until they start to caramelize. Add potatoes and french beans and warm through. Add frisee. Add Ancho Chili Vinaigrette, adjust seasoning.
3. Sear salmon in hot pan and finish in oven for 5 - 8 minutes. Season with salt and pepper.
4. Place a small amount of salad in the middle of a plate, place salmon on top and garnish with reserved sprigs.

Tamarind Glazed Salmon Filet with Green Coconut Curry Jasmine Rice and Spicy Basil Tomato Stir Fry

Serves 4

Tamarind Sauce Ingredients:
1/2 cup Tamarind pod
1/2 cup oyster sauce
1/4 cup shallots
1/4 cup garlic
1/4 cup ginger
1/4 cup lemongrass
1/2 cup soy sauce
1/2 cup ketchup

Green Coconut Curry Jasmine Rice Ingredients:
7 ounce Salmon Filet
cooking oil
salt and pepper
1 tablespoon green curry paste
2 teaspoons garlic, chopped
2 teaspoons shallots, chopped
1/4 cup coconut milk (optional)
4 cups Jasmine rice
black sesame seeds

Spicy Basil Tomato Stir Fry Ingredients:
1 cup sweet Thai chile sauce
1 bunch fresh basil, cut into fine strips
2 large onions, diced
4 roma tomatoes, quartered
2 yellow tomatoes, quartered
1/4 cup wood ear mushroom, julienned
1/2 cup cashews, toasted
snow pea shoots

Continued on next page

Patina
Beaver Creek

1. First prepare Tamarind sauce. In hot pan sauté chopped shallots, garlic, lemongrass and ginger. Add remaining ingredients along with 1 quart water and boil until reduced by 1/2. Cool and reserve.
2. In hot sauté pan, sear salmon filet, seasoning with salt and pepper. Sear other side and add Tamarind sauce over filet until coated.
3. Sweat garlic and shallots in kettle, add 1 tablespoon green curry paste and deglaze with coconut milk if desired. Add jasmine rice with appropriate water until cooked.
4. In smoking hot sauté pan, add 2 tablespoons oil and carefully place onions in pan while stirring vigorously. Add tomatoes when onions are translucent and cook until al dente. Finish with wood ears, cashews, and basil. Deglaze with sweet Thai chile sauce.
5. Place stir fry around plate, jasmine rice in center and salmon on top of rice. Garnish with black sesame seeds and snow peas.

Coriander Encrusted Sea Bass with Red & Yellow Tomato Coulis

Serves 4

Coriander Encrusted Sea Bass Ingredients:

all-purpose flour (for dusting fish)
(4) 6 ounce sea bass filets
salt and pepper to taste
1 tablespoon clarified butter or 1 tablespoon olive oil
3 tablespoons coriander seed
2 bunches fresh spinach, washed, drained & stemmed
1 tablespoon olive oil
Red and yellow tomato Coulis
4 Crispy potato hay stacks

Red Tomato Coulis Ingredients:

1/2 tablespoon olive oil
1 tablespoon shallots, finely chopped
1 clove garlic, finely chopped
4 roma tomatoes, peeled, seeded and diced
1 teaspoon tomato paste
1 cup hot chicken stock
Pinch salt and pepper

Yellow Tomato Coulis Ingredients:

Same ingredients as Red Tomato Coulis, but substitute 2 yellow tomatoes, peeled, seeded and diced and omit tomato paste

Crispy Potato Haystack Ingredients:

Potatoes, cut into 1/4" thick rounds, then cut into matchsticks
Vegetable oil for frying

Continued on next page

Vista Verde Ranch
Steamboat Springs

1. First, prepare each tomato coulis by heating oil in a small sauce pan. Add shallot and garlic and cook 1 minute. Add tomato paste (in Red Tomato Coulis only) and cook for 3 - 5 minutes. Add tomatoes and cook over medium-low heat for 10 minutes. Add stock and continue cooking for 5 - 10 minutes or until tomatoes are very soft.
2. Puree each coulis in a blender or food processor until smooth and then strain. Season with salt and pepper.
3. In 375 degree oil, fry matchstick potatoes. (A deep fryer is optimal, but you may use a large skillet with tall sides and 2" of vegetable oil)
4. Preheat oven to 350 degrees.
5. Place coriander seeds in a sealed plastic bag and crush with meat mallet.
6. Salt and pepper both sides of sea bass. Lightly dust with flour on both sides then roll one side of sea bass in the crushed coriander seeds (one side of the fish is smoother than the other and you want to roll the smooth side in the seeds).
7. Heat a large sauté pan over medium high heat. Add olive oil. When very hot, carefully add the sea bass, coriander side down and cook 4 - 5 minutes. Flip fish over and place in an oven proof pan. Finish cooking in the oven (about 5 more minutes).
8. As fish is finishing, heat another large sauté pan over high heat. Add olive oil and spinach. Quickly toss spinach until just wilted. Season with salt and pepper. Divide spinach among 4 warm plates. Top with fish and garnish with a swirl of Red & Yellow Tomato Coulis. Top fish with a potato haystack.

Grilled Lemon Marinated Swordfish with Roasted Red Pepper Remoulade

Serves 4

Swordfish Ingredients:
4 Swordfish filets or steaks (3/4" thick)
juice of 2 - 3 lemons
salt and pepper to taste

Roasted Red Pepper Remoulade Ingredients:
2 hard boiled eggs
1/2 small red onion
1/2 lime, juice of
2 1/2 cups mayonnaise
1 cup roasted red pepper
capers

1. Mince red onion by hand.
2. Roast pepper in oven or over open flame until skin blackens and blisters. Cool and peel.
3. In a food processor chop roasted red pepper. Add remaining ingredients, (excluding capers) and blend. Add drained capers and mix briefly.
4. Place swordfish filets or steaks in lemon juice for 15 minutes. Grill over hot coals for approximately 4 minutes on each side. Salt and pepper to taste.
5. Serve with dollop of Roasted Red Pepper Remoulade.

The Stonebridge Inn
Snowmass Village

Prosciutto Wrapped Salmon with Gerwurztraminer-Mango Sauce

(6) 6 ounce salmon filets
18 slices prosciutto ham, sliced very thin

Gerwurztraminer Sauce Ingredients:
1 pound ripe mangos, peeled and diced
1 bottle Gewurztraminer wine
1/2 cup honey
2 tablespoons rice wine vinegar
2 tablespoons pink peppercorns

Serves 6

1. Preheat oven to 350 degrees.
2. Wrap each filet with three slices of prosciutto and place in a sauté pan. Bake for 8 - 10 minutes.
3. To make sauce, combine all ingredients, excluding 1/2 of peppercorns, in a 2 quart sauce pan. Bring to boil. Reduce heat to a simmer and stir often for 30 minutes. Transfer to food processor and blend until smooth. Using a rubber spatula, press sauce through a fine mesh strainer. Stir in remaining pepper corns.
4. Pour sauce over salmon and serve.

Aspen's
Aurora

Salmon Tartar

Serves 6

8 ounces salmon, ground
4 ounces smoked salmon, ground
2 tablespoons shallots, chopped
2 teaspoons dill, chopped
2 teaspoons chervil, chopped
2 tablespoons lemon juice
2 tablespoons olive oil
salt and white pepper to taste

1. Place all ingredients in a bowl and mix gently.
2. Shape mixture into quenelles (oval rounds) with 2 soup spoons.
3. Place on salad plate and garnish with chopped egg, minced onion and endive leaves. Serve with toasted brioche.

Ludwig's
Vail

Sesame Crusted Mahi-Mahi with Tomato Wasabi Vinaigrette

Serves 4

Sesame Crusted Mahi-Mahi Ingredients:

24 ounces Mahi-Mahi
2 cups Panko (Japanese bread crumbs)
1 teaspoon white sesame seeds
1 teaspoon black sesame seeds
1 whole egg
flour
salt and pepper to taste
olive oil
lightly sautéed spinach

Tomato Wasabi Vinaigrette Ingredients:

1 cup canned plum tomatoes
1 teaspoon Wasabi powder
1 tablespoon aged sherry vinegar
3 tablespoons extra virgin olive oil
salt and pepper to taste
2 tablespoons fresh chives, chopped

1. Season fish and lightly flour. Dip in lightly beaten egg, then in Panko and sesame seeds.
2. Heat pan with olive oil. Sauté fish on medium heat until brown on both sides and is completely cooked throughout.
3. To prepare vinaigrette, place plum tomatoes, Wasabi powder, sherry vinegar and olive oil in blender or food processor and blend finely. Season to taste and add chives.
4. Place fish on a bed of lightly sautéed spinach. Drizzle with vinaigrette and serve.

Lord Gore Restaurant
Vail

Baked Ruby Red Trout with Chipotle Mashed Potatoes and Roasted Tomato Sauce

Serves 4

Trout Ingredients:
(4) 8 ounce trout filets
2 cups Chipotle Mashed Potatoes
1 bunch red swiss chard
1 1/2 cups Roasted Tomato Sauce

Sauteed Swiss Chard Ingredients:
1 tablespoon butter
1/2 tablespoon garlic, chopped
1/2 cup tomatoes, cut rough
4 cups red swiss chard, cleaned
Kosher salt and black pepper to taste

Chipotle Mashed Potatoes Ingredients:
2 cups russet potatoes, peeled and diced
1/4 cup heavy cream
2 tablespoons butter
1 teaspoon chipotle puree (purchase canned in the mexican food section)
1 egg yolk
Kosher salt and black pepper to taste

Roasted Tomato Sauce Ingredients:
1 medium yellow onion, large dice
4 ripe tomatoes, large dice
1/4 cup garlic cloves, peeled
1/4 olive oil
1 teaspoon Kosher salt
1 teaspoon black pepper
1/2 pound whole butter

Continued on next page

SNOWMASS CLUB™
Sage Restaurant
Snowmass Village

1. Boil potatoes in water until soft enough to mash. In a mixer, with the whip attachment, whip in the remaining ingredients. Season with salt and pepper.
2. Toss all ingredients for Roasted Tomato Sauce, excluding butter, together in a large mixing bowl. Place the mixture on a sheet pan and bake at 375 degrees for 45 minutes or until the onions start to brown and the tomatoes are soft. Place the mixture in a blender and blend in the butter until very smooth.
3. Using a pastry bag with a star tip, pipe the mashed potatoes down the center of the trout filet. Place on greased sheet pan in a 400 degree oven for 7 - 10 minutes.
4. Prepare sautéed swiss chard: In a hot sauce pan melt butter. Add garlic and sauté until soft. Add tomatoes and swiss chard and sauté until the chard is just starting to wilt, leave it a little under cooked so it still has some structure. Season to taste with salt and pepper. (Cook this part of the dish while the trout is in the oven, as it only takes a couple of minutes.)
5. Pour 3 ounces of Roasted Tomato Sauce on the plate. Place the sauteed swiss chard in the center of the plate and place cooked trout filet on top of the swiss chard and serve.

Traditional Spanish Paella

Serves 6

12 large shrimp
1 pound cooked lobster tail in shell
3 pounds skinless chicken pieces
1 tablespoon olive oil
1 Spanish chorizo sausage, thickly sliced
8 ounces cooked ham, cubed
1 red onion, chopped
2 garlic cloves, crushed
2 tomatoes, chopped
2 teaspoons tomato paste
1 cup dry white wine
1 teaspoon saffron threads
2 cups short grain rice
3 cups chicken stock
6 mussels in the shell
1 red bell pepper, sliced
1 cup peas
2 tablespoons parsley, chopped
1 lemon, cut into wedges
herbs, chopped for garnish (parsley, cilantro, basil-your option)

1. Peel and devein shrimp.
2. Heat oil in a casserole dish. Add chicken, chorizo and ham and cook 8 - 10 minutes until golden. Transfer to plate.
3. Add shrimp to pan and sauté about 4 minutes. Transfer shrimp to plate.
4. Preheat oven to 350 degrees.
5. Add onion and garlic to pan and cook until soft. Reduce heat to low, add tomatoes and tomato paste and simmer for 5 minutes.

Continued on next page

Top of the World Restaurant
Breckenridge

6. Heat 1/4 cup of wine in a small sauce pan, add saffron threads and soak for 4 minutes, then strain.
7. Add saffron liquid to onion and tomato mixture. Add rice, stock and remaining wine and boil, stirring continuously. Arrange chicken, chorizo, ham, mussels and red pepper over rice, sprinkle with peas and cover. After baking for 30 minutes, place shrimp and lobsters on top and bake an additional 5 minutes.
8. Garnish with herbs and serve.

Crispy Filet of Colorado Brook Trout with Saffron Mussel Chowder

Serves 4

Saffron Mussel Chowder Ingredients:
12 mussels, scrubbed
1 shallot, finely chopped
1 garlic, crushed
1 cup dry white wine
2 tarragon sprigs
1 lemon, juice of
1 cup fish stock
pinch saffron
juice from mussels
2 tablespoons butter
1 tablespoon all-purpose flour
1 small russet potato, 1/8" cubed
1 tablespoons onion, finely chopped
2 chives, minced
1/8 cup heavy cream

Crispy Filet of Colorado Brook Trout Ingredients:
(2) 4 ounce trout filets with skin
4 tablespoons canola oil
dash salt
dash pepper

1. First combine mussels, shallot, garlic, white wine, 1 tarragon sprig, lemon juice, fish stock and saffron in a shallow sauce pan. Cover with foil. Heat on medium heat until mussels open. Remove from heat and cool.
2. Remove mussels from shells and set aside.
3. Strain liquid and reserve.

Continued on next page

4. In a small sauce pan, melt butter and add onion. Cook until onions are translucent. Add flour and potatoes and cook for 2 - 3 minutes over low heat. Slowly add mussel juice, mixing to make a smooth sauce. Add cream, chopped tarragon and salt and pepper to taste. Simmer gently until potatoes are tender, stirring continuously.
5. To prepare trout, season fish with salt and pepper on both sides. Heat oil over medium heat in a shallow frying pan. (Heat until oil begins to smoke)
6. Place fish in frying pan with the skin side down. Cook for approximately 12 minutes or until fish is crispy and cooked.
7. Serve Mussel Saffron Chowder in a bowl with fish, crispy side on top.

Salmon White Fish Terrine with Curry Vinaigrette

Serves 8

Salmon and White Fish Mixture:
4 pounds salmon, cut into 1" x 1" pieces
4 pounds white fish, cut into 1" x 1" pieces
1/4 pound fresh dill, rough chopped
4 shallots, finely diced
2 garlic, finely diced
1 1/4 cups Aspic (powder)
1/2 cup white wine
1 lemon, juice of
salt and pepper to taste

Curry Vinaigrette Ingredients:
3 cups salad oil
1 1/2 cups honey
1 1/2 cups onions, carrots, celery
1 cup white wine
2 tablespoons curry powder
1 tablespoon turmeric
2 cups chicken stock
2 papaya, diced
1/2 bunch cilantro, chopped
1/2 cup rice wine vinegar
1 tablespoon white wash (equal parts of corn starch and water)
salt and pepper to taste

To make curry vinaigrette:
1. Sauté onion, celery and carrots.
2. Add chicken stock, wine, curry and turmeric and reduce by 1/2.
3. Thicken lightly with white wash and cool.
4. In food processor, mix in vinegar and oil alternately until emulsified.
5. Finish with cilantro, honey, papaya, salt and pepper.

Continued on next page

Augusta
Denver

To make fish mixture:

1. Mix all ingredients together in a bowl.

To assemble:

1. Lay salmon and white fish mixture lengthwise on plastic wrap and roll up like a sausage, then roll tightly in foil.
2. Poach roll in fish stock until cooked to 135 degrees. Place in water bath to cool and refrigerate overnight.
3. Remove fish from plastic and foil and cut into 2 ounce portions. Place on dinner plates with baby mixed greens and top with curry vinaigrette.

Seared Escolar with Pisaladiere, Sorrel Sauce and Red Kale

Serves 4

1 1/2 pounds escolar
1 pound pie or tart dough
2 tablespoons olive oil
1 cup leeks, washed and diced
1 cup yellow onions, julienned
1/2 cup nicoise olives, pitted and chopped
3 tablespoons anchovies, minced
1/2 block silken tofu
2 tablespoons water
1/4 cup salad oil
2 cups sorrel, packed
1 tablespoon lemon juice, or to taste
2 teaspoons sugar
2 teaspoons garlic, chopped
6 cups red Russian kale
salt and pepper to taste

1. Preheat oven to 375 degrees.
2. Cut escolar into 4 equal portions and reserve.
3. Roll tart dough thinly and cut to fit a 9" tart pan, reserving any extra dough for later use. Place fitted tart shell in the freezer to chill.
4. To make tart filling, in a medium sauce pan, over medium-high heat, combine oil, leeks and onions. Cook until caramelized, stirring often, for about 15 minutes. Remove from heat and add olives and anchovy. Reserve.
5. Spread leek mixture atop the chilled tart dough and bake at 375 degrees for 15 - 20 minutes, until browned.
6. To make sauce, combine tofu, water, oil, and sorrel in a blender. Puree until smooth, about 4 minutes. Season to taste with lemon juice, salt and sugar. Reserve.

Continued on next page

Alice's Restaurant
Ward

7. In a large sauté pan over high heat, sauté garlic in small amount of oil, add kale and cook until wilted. Season with salt.
8. In another large sauté pan (or several small ones), sauté escolar for 4 minutes on each side over high heat (medium rare) or until done. Season with salt and pepper.
9. Warm tart, fish and greens in oven if necessary. Divide each among 4 plates and garnish with sorrel sauce. Serve immediately.

Grilled Trout with Fire Roasted Tomato Caper Sauce and Basil Oil

Serves 6

6 trout filets

Fire Roasted Tomato Caper Sauce Ingredients:
10 roma tomatoes
1/3 cup V-8 juice
2 tablespoons capers
1 teaspoon salt
1/2 teaspoon fresh pepper, ground
1 teaspoon fresh parsley, chopped

Basil Oil Ingredients:
1/4 ounce fresh basil, stemmed
3/4 cup light olive oil
1 teaspoon salt
1/2 teaspoon white pepper
1/2 lemon, juice of

1 pound dry linguine

1. Prepare Tomato Caper Sauce: Halve tomatoes lengthwise and grill on both sides on hot BBQ or gas grill.
2. To food processor, add all sauce ingredients, excluding capers and pulse with metal blade until slightly chunky. Add capers and keep warm.
3. Prepare Basil Oil: Combine basil, oil and seasonings in blender and blend until smooth. Transfer to a bottle.
4. Cook pasta until al dente in heavily salted boiling water.
5. Grill trout filets brushed with olive oil and seasoned with salt and pepper.
6. Place linguine in center of plate, drizzle with olive oil, top with trout filet, spoon Tomato Caper Sauce over trout and serve.

COPPER MOUNTAIN RESORT

Pesce Fresco
Copper Mountain

Fresh Tuna Nicoise

1 trout filet, butterflied
2 tablespoons toasted almonds, sliced
4 tablespoons Amaretto liqueur
2 tablespoons butter
2 tablespoons vegetable oil
parsley, chopped for garnish

Serves
1

1. In a medium sauté pan, heat oil over high heat. Place butterflied trout into oil and sauté for 3 minutes each side. Add almonds, Amaretto and butter. Turn off heat and swirl in pan until thickened.
2. Place fish on plate, garnish with chopped parsley and serve.

EVR
Estes Valley Resorts

Aspen Lodge Restaurant
Estes Park

Grilled Filet of Atlantic Salmon with Chive Sauce Presented with Cream Leeks & Asparagus

Serves 6

Salmon Ingredients:
(6) 6 - 7 ounce boneless salmon steaks
salt and pepper to taste
pure olive oil or canola oil

Chive Butter Sauce Ingredients:
1 cup white wine
2 tablespoons shallots, chopped
2 tablespoons champagne vinegar
1 tablespoon coriander, ground
1 pound unsalted butter
4 tablespoons fresh chives
salt and pepper to taste

Creamed Leek and Asparagus Ingredients:
4 leeks, washed and diced
30 - 36 fresh asparagus spears
2 tablespoons whole butter
1 / 2 cup white wine
3 tablespoons capers with vinegar
2 cups heavy cream
salt and pepper to taste

1. Marinate salmon in oil, salt and pepper.
2. Prepare Chive Butter Sauce: On stove, reduce white wine, shallots, vinegar and coriander. Carefully swirl butter into sauce. Combine sauce, chives, salt and pepper in blender and blend on high. Strain mixture and set aside , keeping warm.
3. Prepare Creamed Leeks: Sauté cleaned leeks in butter until translucent. Add white wine and capers. Slightly reduce mixture and add cream. Cook on stove for 2 minutes and season with salt and pepper.

Continued on next page

Top of the World Restaurant
Breckenridge

4. Steam or blanch asparagus.
5. Grill fish to medium texture.
6. Place 5 - 7 asparagus spears in a radial pattern on each plate. Place fish and leeks in the center of the plate. Spoon sauce around the asparagus. Serve with rice or potatoes.

Herb Crusted Salmon on Fresh Spinach Leaves

Serves 4

Herb Crust Ingredients:
1/2 teaspoon dried oregano
1/2 teaspoon dried basil
1/2 teaspoon dried thyme
1/2 teaspoon garlic, minced
1/4 teaspoon salt
1 teaspoon lemon zest
1 1/4 cup bread crumbs

Dressing Ingredients:
1/3 cup olive oil
1/3 cup raspberry vinegar
3 tablespoons sugar
1 pint assorted fresh berries (raspberries & blackberries are great), lightly chopped
1/2 teaspoon black pepper, ground
salt to taste

Salmon Ingredients:
(4) 8 ounce salmon filets, skinned and cleaned
4 italian plum tomatoes, quartered
1/2 red onion, thinly sliced
4 cups fresh spinach leaves, stemmed and cleaned
1/4 cup walnuts, lightly chopped
few drops of olive oil or fresh pesto
Assorted berries for garnish

Continued on next page

Rosso's Ristoranté
Denver

1. In a bowl, combine all the Herb Crust ingredients and set aside.
2. In second bowl, combine the raspberry vinegar, sugar, fresh berries, and pepper. Whisk in the olive oil slowly until combined. Add salt if necessary.
3. Preheat oven to 400 degrees. Grease a large baking dish. Brush salmon with a few drops of olive oil (or pesto) then coat with Herb Crust. Bake salmon for 25 - 30 minutes or until done.
4. On a plate, arrange the fresh spinach leaves, tomatoes, red onions, and top with raspberry vinaigrette. Place salmon on top of spinach leaves, garnish with fresh berries and walnuts.

Mesquite Grilled Salmon over Yellow Pepper Coulis with a Tomato & Cucumber Slaw

Serves 4

Salmon Ingredients:
(4) 8ounce North Atlantic Salmon steaks
1 tablespoon salt
1 teaspoon black pepper, ground
3 tablespoons olive oil

Cous Cous Ingredients:
1 cup cous cous, raw
2 teaspoons cumin
dash salt
1 1/4 cups tomato juice
1/2 tablespoon butter

Tomato and Cucumber Slaw Ingredients:
1 cucumber
2 large tomatoes
1/4 red onion
1 tablespoon lime juice
1 tablespoon rice wine vinegar
2 tablespoons parsley, chopped
2 teaspoons fresh mint, chopped

Yellow Pepper Coulis Ingredients:
1 1/2 pounds yellow peppers, roasted
1 quart cold water
2 teaspoons salt, granulated
1/2 teaspoon white pepper, ground
2 tablespoons rice vinegar, unseasoned
2 ounces lime juice
1 pint heavy cream

Continued on next page

Table Mountain Inn
Golden

1. Prepare Yellow Pepper Coulis: Rub peppers lightly with oil, place on a pan and bake at 350 degrees for 45 minutes or until the skin is dark brown to black. Remove peppers from oven, place in a plastic container and seal for 30 minutes to steam peppers. Remove peppers and peel off the skin. Remove seeds and stems. In a large heavy bottom sauce pan, place peppers, water and salt. Over medium heat, bring to boil, stirring occasionally. Reduce heat to low and simmer, stirring occasionally, for 1 hour. Remove from heat. Puree mixture with blender until very smooth. While blender is running, add white pepper and stream in rice vinegar, then lime juice. Continue blending to incorporate all ingredients. With blender running, stream in heavy cream and mix well. Keep warm.
2. Prepare slaw: Peel cucumber, cut lengthwise and de-seed, cut the halves in half, widthwise, then cut into thin strips lengthwise. Core the tomatoes and cut into thin wedges, about 20 per tomato. Peel and finely dice onion (using only 1/4 of onion). Mix cucumbers, tomatoes, and onions together with rice vinegar, parsley and mint.
3. Prepare cous cous: Pour the tomato juice into a sauce pan, add butter and bring to boil. Once boiling turn the heat off and add spices and cous cous. Cover. Let stand for 8 minutes. Uncover and fluff with a fork. Reserve, keeping warm.
4. Prepare grill with charcoal and mesquite chips.
5. Brush salmon with oil and season with salt and pepper. Place on hot grill and cook to medium rare (or desired temperature).
6. Place the cous cous in the middle of a plate with salmon steak on top and ladle about 3 ounces of the coulis over salmon with a dollop of cucumber slaw on top.

Crab Cakes

Serves
2 - 3

2 1/2 cups bread crumbs (made from sour dough bread without crust)
1/4 stick butter, unsalted
1 cup onion, chopped
1/2 cup celery, chopped
1/2 cup green bell pepper, chopped
1/2 cup fresh parsley, finely chopped
2 teaspoons Worcestershire sauce
1/2 teaspoon fresh garlic, minced
1/4 cup clam juice
1/2 pound lump crab meat or snow crab meat
1 1/2 teaspoons cajun seasoning
1 teaspoon Tabasco sauce
1 large egg, beaten
1/2 cup heavy cream
1/2 cup vegetable oil
olive oil

1. Toast bread crumbs in a skillet over high heat, shaking skillet often, for approximately 1 minute or until bread crumbs are golden brown. Remove from heat and remove crumbs from skillet reserving for later.
2. In the skillet, over high heat, add butter, onions, bell peppers and celery. Cook until vegetables start to soften and brown (3 - 4 minutes), stirring frequently. Add Worcestershire sauce, Tabasco, garlic, cajun seasoning and cook, stirring once or twice, for 2 - 3 minutes. Add clam juice and scrape crust from bottom of skillet then remove from heat.
3. Remove shell and cartilage from lump crab meat.
4. In a small mixing bowl, add the crab meat, toasted bread crumbs, vegetable mixture, egg and cream. Mix together by hand.

Continued on next page

Friar Tuck's Restaurant
Thornton

5. Refrigerate mixture for 1 hour.
6. Measure 1/2 cup of crab mixture and form in a round cake (not too flat).
7. In a skillet, heat oil. When hot, reduce heat to medium-low and add crab cakes. Cook for 2 - 3 minutes on each side.
8. Serve immediately with your favorite sauce or dressing.

Grilled Seabass with Mango Chutney

(4) 6 ounce Seabass filets

Mango Chutney Ingredients:
7 mangos, peeled and diced
1 cup cider vinegar
1/2 cup brown sugar
4 tablespoons raisins
1 tablespoon jalapeño, cleaned and diced
1 clove garlic, diced
1 tablespoon ginger, chopped
1 tablespoon turmeric, ground
1/2 tablespoon nutmeg, ground
1/2 tablespoon allspice, ground
1/2 tablespoon mace, ground
1/2 tablespoon red pepper, ground
1/2 tablespoon salt

Serves 4

1. Prepare Mango Chutney: Simmer mango in cider vinegar for 10 minutes. Add sugar and raisins, simmer 5 minutes. Add jalapeño, garlic and ginger and simmer 5 minutes. Add spices and simmer an additional 5 minutes.
2. Season Seabass with salt and pepper and grill to desired doneness.
3. Serve Seabass with dollop of Mango Chutney on top.

Garden Terrace
Englewood

Beef & Game Entrees

Housemade Elk Pastrami, Red Cabbage & Fennel Sauerkraut

elk leg meat
corn brine
pepper, fresh ground
coriander, fresh ground
fennel seed, fresh ground
caraway seed, fresh ground

Serves 12

Sauerkraut Ingredients:
sweet onion, thinly sliced
red cabbage, thinly sliced
fennel, thinly sliced
caraway seeds
star anise
dark beer
chicken stock
lemon juice
salt and pepper

1. Cure the elk in the brine for 3 days. Make sure the meat is fully submerged, turning twice a day. Remove from cure and rinse under cold water, pat dry. Crust with fresh ground spice mixture and smoke with mesquite wood chips for 30 minutes. Finish in an oven until done. Cool and slice thin.
2. Add all sauerkraut ingredients in a cold pot (anise and caraway should be placed in a sachet), cover and place on low heat. Stir every 30 minutes. Braise until liquid is gone.

THE WESTIN
TABOR CENTER

Augusta
Denver

Filet Herbert

Serves 4

2 tablespoons olive oil
(4) 8 ounce filet of beef tenderloin
3 tablespoons Cognac
1 cup Major Grey's Chutney
fresh ground pepper
salt
3 tablespoons beef stock (canned beef broth can be used)

1. Pre-heat sauté pan over medium heat. Add olive oil. Sear tenderloins about 2 to 3 minutes being careful not to scorch. Remove tenderloin from pan.
2. Add Cognac to sauté pan and stir until warm. Return tenderloins and deglaze. Add Major Grey's Chutney, lots of fresh ground black pepper (about 20 turns of the pepper mill), a pinch of salt and beef stock. Continue to cook tenderloins to desired doneness. While meat finishes cooking the sauce will reduce to a nice savory sauce.
3. Serve the filets on a plate with your favorite pasta or fresh garden vegetable. Cover each filet with about 2 - 3 ounces of sauce.

Henry's Italian Bistro
Durango

Grilled Filet Mignon: Mesquite Seasoned & Wrapped in Peppered Bacon with Onion Marmalade and Cheese-herb Grits

Serves 1

(1) 8 ounce filet, grilled to your liking
2 slices peppered bacon
mesquite seasoning (any brand)

Onion Marmalade Ingredients:
1 medium yellow onion, julienned

Herb-Cheese Grits Ingredients:
1 cup water
3 tablespoons grits
salt (optional)
4 tablespoons Cheddar cheese
fresh rosemary, oregano, thyme

Melba Sauce Ingredients:
1/2 cup raspberry jam
1 cup raspberries
1 teaspoon corn starch
1/2 cup sugar

1. To prepare melba sauce, combine raspberry jam and raspberries then add corn starch and sugar. Cook over boiling until thick and clear. Strain through sieve and chill.
2. Slowly stir grits and salt into boiling water. Reduce heat to medium-low and cook until thickened. Add Cheddar cheese, rosemary, oregano and thyme.
3. Spread mixture on to a flat surface (cake pan) and cool. Once cooled, cut into squares and cook in a small amount of butter until brown on both sides.
4. Sauté onion over medium heat until transparent. Add melba sauce and simmer for 5 minutes.
5. Grill filet to your taste.

The Edgewater Grille
Durango

orado Free Range Venison with Blue Cheese Foie Gras Souffle in Hazelnut Game Jus

Serves 2

(2) 4 ounce medallions of venison
1 tablespoon flour
1 tablespoon foie gras
1/2 tablespoon whole butter
1/2 tablespoon Roquefort cheese
1/4 cup whole milk
1 egg, separated
1 rosemary sprig, chopped
1/2 clove garlic
1 shallot, chopped
dash salt
dash pepper

Sauce Ingredients:
2 tablespoons Frangelica liqueur
2 tablespoons dry red wine
1 shallot, chopped
1 rosemary sprig
1 tablespoon balsamic vinegar
1/2 cup game stock

1. Prepare sauce: Combine shallots, rosemary, vinegar and reduce by 2/3. Add 1/2 cup game stock and reduce by 1/2. Strain and finish with Frangelica. Salt and pepper to taste.
2. Sear the venison medallions in a pan for approximately 2 minutes on each side. Refrigerate until cold.
3. Wrap the base of the medallion in a 2" x 6" piece of buttered parchment paper creating a pillar-like effect.
4. Melt butter and add foie gras over low heat until it's fat is rendered. Add shallot and garlic and sweat until translucent. Mix in flour to make a roux, slowly adding the milk until it is a creamy paste. Fold in softened Roquefort and

Continued on next page

rosemary until it becomes smooth. Season with salt and pepper and refrigerate until cool.

5. Once cool, add egg yolk. Beat the white separately and fold into soufflé base. Split the mix into two batches placing it on top of the parchment wrapped venison.
6. Bake at 425 degrees for 20 minutes until the soufflé is done and the venison is medium rare.

Tequila Beef Burritos

Serves 4

2 pounds flank steak, sliced thin
1/2 cup oil
2 tablespoons chili powder
2 teaspoons cumin
1/2 cup tequila
2 limes, juice of
1 tablespoon garlic
refried beans
lettuce, shredded
tomatoes, diced
Cheddar cheese, shredded
2 tablespoons salsa
sour cream
guacamole
flour tortillas

1. Mix oil, chili powder, cumin, tequila, lime juice and garlic. Place sliced beef into a 1-gallon Ziplock bag and pour marinade on the beef. Seal, letting the air escape and marinate in the refrigerator for a least 6 hours, turning the bag over every couple of hours.
2. After marinating, cook beef on a grill or in a sauté pan.
3. Heat tortilla shells.
4. Spread refried beans on 1/3 of the tortilla. Place 8 ounces of cooked meat on the beans and roll.
5. Serve with lettuce, tomatoes, cheese, salsa, sour cream and guacamole.

Best Western Executive Inn
The Cockpit Grille
Denver

Buffalo Stroganoff

Serves 4

1 pound buffalo stew meat, cubed
1 onion, diced
1 celery stalk, diced
1 leek, diced
1/2 cup pearl onions
1 bay leaf
2 teaspoons black pepper
2 teaspoons paprika
2 teaspoons thyme
1 tablespoon salt
2 tablespoons vegetable oil

Sauce Ingredients:
3/4 cup red wine
4 tablespoons brandy
1 cup Shiitake mushrooms, sliced
1 cup button mushrooms, sliced
2 garlic cloves, minced
1 tablespoon tomato paste
3/4 cup canned whole peeled tomatoes
3 cups beef broth
1/4 cup sour cream

1. In medium sauce pan brown buffalo in vegetable oil. Add pearl onions and brown well. Add remaining vegetables and spices and cook for 10 minutes.
2. Deglaze pan with brandy and red wine. Add remaining ingredients and simmer for 2 - 3 hours until the meat is tender. Remove from heat.
3. Add sour cream and mix well.
4. Serve over buttered noodles and garnish with chopped scallions, tomatoes and sour cream.

SNOWMASS CLUB

Sage Restaurant
Snowmass Village

Red Deer Mignon with Ginger & Lemon Broccoli Mousseline

Serves 4

(4) 6 ounce pieces red deer tenderloin
1 lemon
1 gingeroot
3 tablespoons sugar
1 tablespoon honey
1 tablespoon red wine vinegar
1 cup fresh orange juice
6 tablespoons butter
2 heads broccoli
2 tablespoons virgin olive oil
3 tablespoons sugar
salt and pepper to taste

1. Peel zest from lemon and julienne. Blanch twice.
2. Peel gingeroot (save peels) and julienne. Blanch twice.
3. In a sauce pan, combine lemon zest and ginger in water to cover. Add sugar and cook until tender. Strain and set aside.
4. In a sauce pan, combine honey, vinegar and ginger peel. Reduce over medium heat to 1 teaspoon. Add orange juice and reduce to 1/4 cup. Add butter. Pour mixture into blender and blend for 1 minute. Strain and keep hot.
5. Cook broccoli in salted boiling water until tender. Drain and puree in a food processor. Add olive oil and keep hot.
6. Sauté red deer in butter until medium rare (do not overcook). Season with salt and pepper.
7. Place 2 tablespoons of Broccoli Mousseline and a piece of red deer on each of four hot plates. Pour sauce over deer and garnish with julienned lemon zest and ginger.

Elk Maison

(3) 2 ounce pieces elk
1 1/2 teaspoons shallots
4 tablespoons mushrooms
4 tablespoons Madiera wine
1/2 cup heavy cream
2 tablespoons butter
2 tablespoons vegetable oil

Serves 1

1. With a meat tenderizer, pound each piece of elk until thin.
2. In a medium sauté pan heat oil over high heat. Place scallopini of elk in the oil. Sauté for 1 minute each side and set aside.
3. In the same sauté pan, add sliced mushrooms and sauté until tender. Add Madiera wine, heavy cream, and butter. Reduce to desired consistency.
4. Serve elk on dinner plate and pour sauce and mushrooms over top.

EVR
Estes Valley Resorts

Aspen Lodge Restaurant
Estes Park

Sherry's Barbeque Brisket

Serves 10

5 - 6 pound brisket
1/4 cup water
1 large onion, peeled and sliced
(1) 8 ounce bottle chili sauce
4 cloves garlic, peeled and chopped
2 bay leaves
1/2 cup brown sugar
1/3 cup dijon mustard
1/4 cup red wine vinegar
3 tablespoons molasses
1/4 cup soy sauce

1. Preheat oven to 325 degrees with the rack in the lower third, but not bottom, position.
2. Sear the meat, fat side down first, in the bottom of a heavy-duty roasting pan. Turn meat over and sear the other side. This searing can also be done on the grill.
3. Stir together all ingredients and pour over brisket. Cover and cook for 3 - 4 hours or until tender.
4. Remove the meat from the pan and pour the sauce into a bowl. Discard bay leaves.
5. Cool broth. Slice meat when cool.
6. Skim the fat off the sauce, then pour back over the sliced meat. Reheat on the stove or in the oven.
7. Serve with lemon carrots, mashed potatoes, rolls and garnish with parsley.

Elk Mountain Guest Ranch
Buena Vista

Carne Adovada

1/2 pound pork, diced
1 pound beef, diced
1 cup onion, diced
1 tablespoon garlic, minced
2 cups red chile puree (hot or mild)
1 cup chicken stock
salt and pepper to taste

Serves 4

1. Brown pork and beef in a heavy skillet. Add garlic and onion and sauté until translucent. Add red chile and chicken stock and simmer until meat is tender (should have the consistency of stew). Season with salt and pepper.
2. Serve with flour tortillas and Cheddar cheese.

Foothills Restaurant
Denver

Colorado Farm Raised Elk Loin Marinated in Juniper Berries & Cognac

Serves 4

Marinade Ingredients:
2 pounds elk
6 tablespoons juniper berries
2 bay leaves
6 sprigs fresh thyme
4 sprigs rosemary
2 cups olive oil
4 tablespoons Cognac
cracked black pepper

Celery Puree Ingredients:
3 celeriac
1 potato
2 cups cream
salt and pepper to taste

Black-Currant Sauce Ingredients:
silver skin
1 cup fresh cassis
1 cup sugar
1 cup water
1 cup red wine vinegar
2 quarts elk stock
1/2 cup roasted pine nuts for garnish
1/2 cup fresh cassis for garnish

1. Clean up the elk loin by taking the silver skin away. Cut into (4) 6 ounces pieces.
2. Marinate the elk loin with cracked juniper berries, cracked black pepper, bay leaves, rosemary, olive oil and cognac for a few hours.
3. Use all the silver skin from the loin and roast them in a sauté pan. When golden

Continued on next page

The Antlers
Durango

brown, add sugar and water, let caramelize then deglaze with red wine vinegar and 1 cup fresh cassis. Reduce until syrup consistency, then add elk stock. Let cook for 45 minutes and strain.

4. Cook celeriac and potato in water and salt. When cooked, puree in blender, add cream, salt and pepper and keep in a warm place.
5. Roast the elk in a sauté pan until medium rare. Place the celeriac puree in the middle of the plate surrounded with the sliced loin, the sauce and garnish with fresh black currants and roasted pine nuts.

Pan Seared Filet Medallions on a bed of Caramelized Onions with a Balsamic Glaze

1 pound of 2 ounce beef tenderloins
1 1/2 cups Balsamic vinegar
2 teaspoons brown sugar
2 large yellow onions, julienned
1/4 cup canola oil and olive oil blend
salt and pepper to taste

Serves 4

1. Trim and cut tenderloin into 2 ounce medallions.
2. In a small sauce pan, reduce the Balsamic vinegar until it becomes a syrupy glaze. Add the brown sugar to taste to sweeten the glaze. Set aside and keep warm.
2. In a medium sauce pan, add 1/2 of the cooking oil and add onions. Sauté over high heat until golden brown. Stir the onions often so they do not burn and add a touch of salt and pepper to season. After onions are caramelized, set aside and keep warm.
3. In a large sauté pan, heat the remaining oil until the pan is slightly smoking. Carefully lay the filet medallions in the pan. Season with salt and pepper. After about one minute, turn the medallions over and cook for one more minute or two depending on your desired temperature.
4. Lay down a bed of caramelized onions on a dinner plate, place 3 medallions on top and brush them with the Balsamic glaze.

Grand Lake Lodge
Grand Lake

Lamb, Pork & Veal Entrees

Mountain Honey & Cumin Roasted Colorado Rack of Lamb with Sweet Garlic Rosemary Jus

8 bones rack of lamb
2 tablespoons canola oil

Glaze Ingredients:
1 1/2 teaspoons unsalted butter
2 tablespoons Colorado Mountain Honey
2 sprigs rosemary, chopped
1/2 teaspoon cumin, ground
dash salt
dash pepper

Sauce Ingredients:
1/4 cup Dry Vermouth
1 shallot, finely chopped
1/2 teaspoon garlic, roasted
1 cup beef broth
1 sprig rosemary

Serves 4

1. Melt the butter and add cumin and rosemary. Cook on gentle heat for 2 minutes. Add honey, salt and pepper. Bring to a boil. Remove and cool to room temperature.
2. Pan fry the lamb on all sides until golden brown, using canola oil over gentle heat. In same pan, place the lamb in a 425 degree oven. Roast the lamb until instant read thermometer reads 125 degrees at the center of the meat for medium rare. Brush with glaze and bake for an additional 2 minutes. Remove lamb from oven, then remove from pan and let rest for 10 minutes.
3. Using the lamb pan (with excess grease removed) add all of the sauce ingredients, excluding the broth. When the mixture has reduced by 3/4, add the broth then reduce by half. Strain the sauce with a fine sieve.
4. Carve the rack of lamb, sauce the meat and serve.

Charles Court
Colorado Springs

Veal Stuffed with Panchetta Smoked Gouda

Serves 4 - 6

1 pound panchetta, sliced extra thin
1 pound smoked Gouda, sliced thin
2 cups veal demi glace
1 large Portobello mushroom, sliced
2 shallots, minced
1 bulb fresh garlic, topped & roasted until soft and sweet
4 - 6 pieces fresh veal medallions, pounded thin
1 cup port
4 tablespoons butter
1/2 cup roux (3 tablespoons flour, 3 tablespoons butter, cooked together)

1. Lay 1 piece of veal on a cutting board. Lay 4 ounces of panchetta to cover the entire piece of veal without going over the edge. Repeat with the Gouda. Carefully roll the veal, panchetta, Gouda into a log form. Take one foot of butcher's twine and tie off the end and wrap the piece of veal to the other end. Tie and cut remaining twine. Repeat with the other pieces of veal.
2. In a lightly oiled sauté pan, braise veal until golden. Drain excess oil and place in a 350 degree oven until cooked to 130 degrees. Let rest for 5 minutes.
3. In a pan melt butter and add Portobello, shallots, and garlic. Sauté until tender. Add port and reduce by 1/2. Add veal demi glace and bring to a heavy simmer. Add roux until a good consistency. Salt and pepper to taste.
4. Untie each veal log and slice 3 or 4 pieces. Cover with sauce and serve.

C Lazy U Ranch
Granby

Lamb Shank Ragout

Serves 6

5 pounds of lamb shanks
1 1/4 quarts lamb stock (beef stock can be substituted)
1/2 fava beans, shucked
1 1/8 cups tomato concasse
7/8 teaspoon rosemary, chopped
7/8 teaspoon thyme, chopped
7/8 teaspoon oregano, chopped
7/8 teaspoon sage, chopped
7/8 teaspoon marjoram, chopped
1 1/8 cups burgundy
salt and pepper to taste
1/2 cup flour
1/3 cup vegetable oil
1/2 cup bay leaf

1. Season lamb shanks with salt and pepper and dip them in flour.
2. Heat oil in a shallow stock pot.
3. Brown the shanks on all sides, deglaze with the burgundy. Reduce the wine by half and add the lamb stock. Add bay leaf and bring to a boil. Cover the pot and place in the oven at 325 degrees for approximately 3 minutes or until the meat is falling off of the bones. Remove the shanks and let cool.
4. Pull all the meat off of the bones and put back in the sauce. Simmer until the sauce thickens naturally. Add tomatoes, fava beans and chopped herbs. Season with salt and pepper if necessary.

Ludwig's
Vail

Grilled Colorado Lamb T-bone with Butternut Squash, Cinnamon-Cap Mushrooms & Potato Gnocchi

Serves 4

Red Wine Lamb Jus Ingredients:
2 pounds lamb bones, cut in small pieces
1 white onion, roughly chopped
1/2 head garlic
2 roma tomatoes, quartered
1 sprig parsley
3 sprigs thyme
2 cups red zinfandel wine
3 cups chicken stock

Potato Gnocchi Ingredients:
4 medium potatoes, cleaned and pierced
1 egg yolk
1 cup all-purpose flour
1/2 teaspoon salt

Butternut Squash & Mushrooms Ingredients:
1 butternut squash, roasted and diced
1 cup cinnamon cap mushrooms, sauteed
1/2 lemon
4 tablespoons butter
4 fresh sage leaves, chiffonade

8 lamb T-bones

Continued on next page

The Wildflower
Vail

1. Place lamb bones into a medium sauce pot and roast in a preheated 350 degree oven. Roast until thoroughly browned. Add onion, tomato and herbs and continue to roast for 10 minutes. Place the sauce pot on top of the stove and add red zinfandel and reduce by half. Add chicken stock and simmer until one cup of the jus remains. Strain and reserve jus liquid for presentation.
2. Bake potatoes in a preheated 350 degree oven until cooked. Remove from oven and cut in half. Scoop out the flesh of the potato and rice the potato meat. Place potato meat on counter and make a well in the center of the pile. Sprinkle with salt, add egg yolk and begin to knead in the flour, 1/4 cup at a time. When the dough comes together, let it rest for 2 minutes. Roll the dough into 1/2" logs. Cut each log into 1/2" pieces, place on floured sheet tray and set aside.
3. To prepare squash and mushrooms, heat the butter in a small sauté pan until brown. Squeeze in lemon juice, add sage, butternut squash and mushrooms. Toss together over low heat and season with salt and pepper.
4. Season the T-bones with salt and pepper. Grill the lamb on each side for 3 minutes. Remove from grill and place in a pan. Place in preheated 350 degree oven until medium rare (4 - 5 minutes).
5. Boil salted water, place the potato gnocchi into a pasta basket and submerge in the boiling water until they float. When cooked, place the gnocchi into the sauté pan with the squash and mushrooms. Toss together until evenly mixed.
6. Heat the reserved lamb jus.
7. Place 2 cooked lamb T-bones into the center of each serving bowl. Equally divide the potato gnocchi mixture into each bowl. Spoon 1 1/2 ounces of the lamb jus evenly over each portion. Serve immediately.

Seared Veal Sirloin

Serves 6

1 1/2 pounds veal sirloin
12 slices bacon

Sauce Ingredients:
1 cup veal stock, reduced
1 shallot, finely chopped
1/8 cup lemon juice
1/8 cup cilantro, chopped
1 red pepper, diced
salt and pepper to taste

Black Bean Chili Ingredients:
1/2 pound black beans
1/3 cup extra virgin olive oil
1 teaspoon garlic, finely chopped
1 medium yellow onion, diced
1 jalapeño chile pepper, diced
1 red bell pepper, diced
1 green bell pepper, diced
1 tomato, diced
1/4 cup lime juice
1/8 cup cilantro, chopped
2 teaspoons chili powder
1 teaspoon cumin
salt and pepper to taste

Continued on next page

Capers Bistro
Denver

1. Soak black beans overnight.
2. Bring veal stock to a simmer. Add shallot, lemon juice, cilantro and red pepper. Sauce can be thickened with corn starch and water if desired.
3. Cut veal into 2 ounce medallions and wrap a slice of bacon around each medallion. Season with salt and pepper and sear in a very hot pan. Cook until desired temperature and set aside.
4. Bring beans to a boil. Reduce heat and cook until tender. Drain.
5. Sauté garlic, onions, and peppers in olive oil. Do not brown or over cook.
6. Add vegetables to black beans and stir in lime juice, cilantro, chili powder and cumin. Season with salt and pepper.
7. Place 2 veal medallions on dinner plate and cover with black bean chili. Serve immediately.

Rack of Lamb Chops with Oven Roasted Vegetables

rack of lamb, french cut

Marinade Ingredients:
2 cloves garlic, minced
1 teaspoon cracked black pepper
Serves 6 - 8
1/3 cup pure olive oil
rosemary
thyme
chervil
parsley
bay leaf
oregano
basil

Oven Dried Tomato Ingredients:
10 roma tomatoes
olive oil

Oven Roasted Vegetable Ingredients:
1 large eggplant
3 medium zucchini, diced
1 large yellow onion, diced
1 cup button mushrooms, quartered
2 cloves garlic, minced
1 cup olive oil
1 tablespoon parsley
1/2 teaspoon thyme
1/2 teaspoon oregano
1/2 tablespoon black pepper
1/2 teaspoon salt

Continued on next page

The Garden Room
Keystone

1. Combine marinade ingredients. Marinate rack of lamb in a ziplock bag overnight.
2. Cut roma tomatoes in half, lengthwise, and seed. Coat with olive oil and spread out on a sheet pan. Bake at 175 degrees for 2 hours until tomatoes are leathery in texture.
3. Peel eggplant and cut into large dice. Transfer to a bowl, sprinkle with salt and let stand 1 hour. Press out any accumulated liquid. Combine eggplant with remaining roasted vegetable ingredients and mix well. Spread on a sheet pan and roast at 300 degrees for 1 hour, stirring occasionally.
4. Dice oven dried tomatoes and combine with other vegetables. Keep warm.
5. Cut lamb into chops and grill.
6. Place vegetables in middle of plate and surround with lamb rack chops and serve.

Grilled Lamb with Tomato Pearl Cous Cous

Serves 8

Port Demi Glaze Ingredients:
4 tablespoons shallots, chopped
4 tablespoons garlic, chopped
1 tablespoon fresh rosemary with stem
1 tablespoon fresh thyme with stem
3 cups port wine
2 cups red wine
1 pint fresh raspberries
4 cups veal stock
1/2 teaspoon salt
1/4 teaspoon pepper
4 tablespoons unsweetened butter

Tomato Pearl Cous Cous Ingredients:
4 cups Israeli cous cous
4 cups chicken stock
1/4 teaspoon salt
1/4 teaspoon pepper
1 teaspoon fresh parsley, chopped
1 teaspoon fresh sage, chopped
1 medium tomato, chopped
1 teaspoon tomato paste

Lamb Chop Ingredients:
16 lamb T-bones
4 tablespoons parsley, chopped
3 tablespoons sage, chopped
1 tablespoon thyme, chopped
1/2 cup whole grain mustard
8 rosemary sprigs
16 baby carrots, peeled
1 large red beet, peeled

Continued on next page

Colorado's Ski-in Ski-out Hotel℠

The Brothers' Grille
Snowmass Village

Lamb Chop Ingredients, continued:

32 asparagus, cleaned and trimmed
1 teaspoon shallots, chopped
1 teaspoon garlic, chopped
4 tablespoons unsweetened butter
1 teaspoon salt
1 teaspoon pepper

1. To prepare the port demi glaze, put the first 7 ingredients in a sauce pot and bring to a boil. Reduce the heat to a simmer and reduce by half. Add the veal stock, salt and pepper and let reduce until the viscosity will coat the back of a spoon. Finish with butter.
2. To prepare the cous cous, heat the chicken stock and dissolve the tomato paste, then bring to a boil. Pour the chicken stock mixture over the cous cous in a baking pan. Add the rest of the ingredients and mix. Cover with aluminum foil and set aside for 15 minutes or until the liquid is absorbed.
3. Blanch carrots and asparagus to al denté. Melt butter and sauté the garlic and shallots until aromatic. Add vegetables to melted butter mixture and season with salt and pepper. Sauté until done.
4. Rub the whole grain mustard on both sides of the lamb T-bones and pat on chopped herbs. Grill to desired temperature.
5. Place 2 T-bones on each plate with cous cous and the vegetables and garnish with rosemary sprigs and sliced beets.

Poultry Entrees

Caribbean Paella

Serves 4

1 pound chicken, julienned
1/2 pound andoulli sausage, sliced
2 1/4 teaspoons olive oil
1/2 onion, julienned
2/3 red bell pepper, julienned
2/3 green bell pepper, julienned
2 3/8 teaspoons garlic
1/4 can chopped clams
3/4 cup arborio rice
1 5/8 pints chicken stock
1/4 can chopped tomatoes
3/4 bay leaf
2 3/8 teaspoons oregano, dry
2 3/8 teaspoons basil, dry
1 3/4 teaspoons cumin
1 1/4 teaspoons cayenne pepper
1/8 bottle Worcestershire sauce
7/8 teaspoon file powder
salt and pepper to taste

1. Sauté meat with olive oil. Add vegetables and cook until soft. Add rice, all liquid and spices and cook for 30 minutes.
2. Cool and serve.

Centennial Restaurant
Denver

Chicken and Artichoke

Serves 4

4 chicken breasts
2 tablespoons margarine

Sauce Ingredients:
(1) 14 ounce can of artichoke hearts, quartered
4 tablespoons margarine
1 cup mushrooms, sliced
2 tablespoons flour
1 cup chicken broth
1/4 cup white wine
1 teaspoon salt
1/2 teaspoon paprika
1/4 teaspoon pepper

1. Sauté chicken in margarine until lightly browned. Place in baking dish and arrange artichoke hearts on top.
2. Sauté mushrooms in margarine. Stir in flour and cook for 2 minutes. Add chicken broth, white wine, salt, paprika and pepper and stir. Cook until thickened.
3. Pour sauce over chicken and artichokes. Bake, uncovered, at 350 degrees for 45 minutes.

Latigo Ranch
Kremmling

Duck with Raspberry-Pepperoncini Sauce

(8) 6 ounce boneless duck breasts
1 cup pepperoncinis, chopped with juice
1 cup raspberry liqueur
1 cup raspberry preserves
1 cup fresh or frozen raspberries
1 cup sugar

Serves 4

1. Mix all ingredients, excluding duck breasts, in a sauce pan and simmer for 30 minutes. Stir occasionally to prevent sauce from sticking.
2. Grill duck breasts, skin side down, for 10 minutes (until skin is crisp). Flip breasts over and grill for another 6 - 12 minutes, depending on your temperature preference.
3. Slice each breast into four pieces at a 45 degree angle and top with raspberry sauce. Garnish with one whole pepperoncini and some fresh raspberries.

C Lazy U Ranch
Granby

Chicken Piccata with Lemon Caper Butter Sauce

Serves 4

(4) 6 ounce chicken breasts, cut in half

Marinade Ingredients:
2 tablespoons lemon or lime juice
6 tablespoons Chablis
2 tablespoons virgin olive oil
2 sprigs tarragon, chopped
1/2 teaspoon Kosher salt
dash of white pepper, ground

Lemon Caper Butter Sauce Ingredients:
2 tablespoons lemon or lime juice
4 tablespoons Chablis
1/2 cup brown chicken stock
2 tablespoons virgin olive oil
2 tablespoons unsalted butter
2 tablespoons shallots, peeled and diced
1 clove garlic, peeled and chopped
2 tablespoons capers, roughly chopped
salt and pepper to taste

angel hair pasta
lemon grass, chopped
tomatoes, chopped
cilantro, chopped

1. Combine all marinade ingredients in a shallow pan and place the chicken breasts in to marinate. Keep in cool place for approximately 10 minutes.
2. Remove the chicken from the marination and sauté each breast in olive oil on both sides until they are well done. Remove from pan and set aside.
3. Sweat shallots and garlic in butter. Add capers and deglaze with chablis. Reduce for approximately 1 minute. Add lemon juice and chicken stock and simmer for 2 minutes.
4. Serve over angel hair pasta with lemon grass and drizzle the chicken with the caper-lemon sauce. Garnish with diced tomatoes and chopped cilantro.

Tavern
Colorado Springs

Roast Breast of Chicken with Focaccia Lemon Sage Stuffing

4 chicken breast with skin on
2 tablespoons butter

Focaccia Crouton Ingredients:
1 focaccia loaf, cut into cubes
1 cup olive oil

Serves 4

Focaccia Stuffing Ingredients:
2 cloves garlic, minced
2 tablespoons olive oil
2 tablespoons shallots, minced
2 lemons, juice of
1/2 cup chopped fresh sage
3 cups chicken stock
2 teaspoons salt
1 teaspoon black pepper

1. Coat focaccia cubes with olive oil and minced garlic. Spread on sheet pan and bake at 350 degrees until cubes are crunchy like croutons.
2. In a large skillet, sauté shallots in olive oil until golden then add lemon juice, sage, chicken stock, salt, pepper, and 8 cups focaccia croutons. Continue to cook on stovetop until liquid is absorbed and cubes break up. Cover with foil and bake at 300 degrees for 30 minutes.
3. Place stuffing between skin and flesh of chicken breast and sear in skillet on both sides. Roast in oven at 350 degrees until chicken is done. Remove from pan and bring juices to simmer. Season and stir in 2 tablespoons whole butter.

The Garden Room
Keystone

Grilled Honey Marinated Squab Breast

Serves 4

4 boneless squab breasts

Honey Marinade Ingredients:
1/4 cup olive oil
2 tablespoons honey
1 sprig thyme
1 shallot, sliced
2 teaspoons black pepper, ground

Walnut Vinaigrette Ingredients:
2 tablespoons sherry vinegar
1/4 cup extra virgin olive oil
1 tablespoon walnut oil
1 tablespoon maple syrup
1/2 tablespoon shallot, finely diced

Arugula Salad Ingredients:
4 cups arugula, washed and dried
20 walnuts, halved and toasted
28 dried cranberries

1. Heat marinade ingredients in a sauce pot, over low heat, for 2 minutes. Pour marinade over squab breasts. Allow to marinate for 2 hours in the refrigerator.
2. To prepare walnut vinaigrette, add shallots and vinegar to a mixing bowl and let sit for 30 minutes. Add the maple syrup and whisk in the oils. Season with salt and pepper.
3. Preheat oven to 350 degrees.
4. Season the marinated squab breasts with salt and pepper. Grill the breasts, skin side first, for 1 minute. Turn and grill the other side for 1 minute. Remove

Continued on next page

The Wildflower
Vail

from the grill and place in a pan. Place in oven and bake until medium rare (3 - 4 minutes).

5. Place the arugula in a mixing bowl with the toasted walnuts, dried cranberries and 1/4 cup Walnut Vinaigrette. Mix the salad and add more dressing if desired.
6. Equally divide the salad onto 4 plates. Cut the squab breasts in half and place one breast on top of each salad. Serve immediately.

Chicken Cilantro

Serves 1

2 tablespoons onion, diced
1/4 clove garlic
1 tablespoon margarine
1 tablespoon oil
1 skinless chicken breast, diced to 1" pieces
pinch salt
pinch black pepper
1/4 cup fresh cilantro, snipped
6 tablespoons rice, cooked
6 tablespoons vegetables, steamed

1. In a 10" skillet, cook onions and garlic in margarine and oil until onion is tender. Add chicken, salt and pepper and cook over medium-high heat until done (about 5 minutes). Stir in cilantro and cook an additional minute.
2. Serve on hot plate. Pour pan juice over chicken. Garnish with lemon.

Garden Terrace
Colorado Springs

Burgundy Braised Chicken Breast Puttanesca

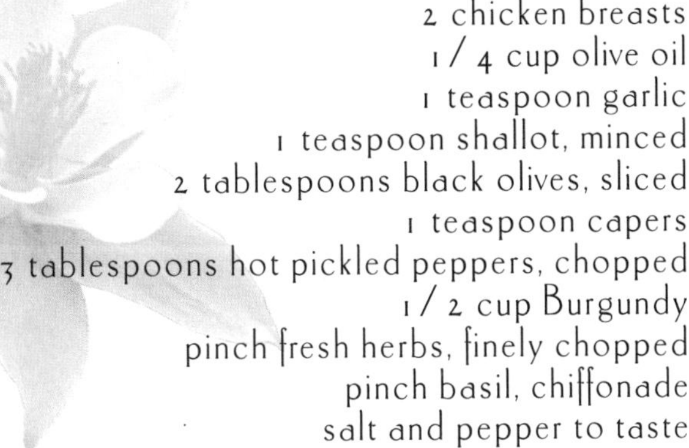

2 chicken breasts
1/4 cup olive oil
1 teaspoon garlic
1 teaspoon shallot, minced
2 tablespoons black olives, sliced
1 teaspoon capers
3 tablespoons hot pickled peppers, chopped
1/2 cup Burgundy
pinch fresh herbs, finely chopped
pinch basil, chiffonade
salt and pepper to taste

Serves 2

1. Heat oil and brown chicken. Add remaining ingredients and place in 350 degree oven for 10 minutes. Remove from oven.
2. Serve chicken on a bed of pasta of your choice.

Centennial Restaurant
Denver

Chicken Piccata

(4) 6 ounce chicken breasts
1 teaspoon capers
1/2 cup heavy cream
1 cup seasoned flour
1/2 ounce lemon juice
1/2 ounce white wine

Serves 4

1. Lightly flour chicken breasts.
2. Heat a small amount of oil in a sauté pan and sauté chicken on both sides until they are just about cooked. Remove and hold.
3. Drain oil from pan, return to heat and add capers, lemon juice and white wine. Cook until reduced by half. Slowly add heavy cream. Return chicken breasts to sauce and continue cooking for 3 - 5 minutes.
4. Serve with pasta and fresh vegetables.

Best Western Executive Inn
The Cockpit Grille
Denver

Breast of Chicken with Morel Mushro

4 chicken breasts
1 cup chablis
1 cup fresh mushrooms
1 quart heavy cream
salt and pepper to taste
sprigs of fresh parsley

Serves 4

1. Bone out chicken breasts and remove skins. Season with salt and pepper.
2. Sauté the chicken in a preheated fry pan with butter for approximately 5 minutes on each side. Place in 250 degree oven to keep warm.
3. Remove grease from pan and deglaze with chablis. Boil down to half then add mushrooms. Reduce a little more and add heavy cream seasoned with salt and pepper. Reduce by half again. Sauce should be thick.
4. Remove breasts from oven and place on hot plates. Cover with sauce and mushrooms. Garnish with sprigs of fresh parsley and serve with new potatoes and julienned vegetables.

Andre's Bistro
Avon

Pan-Roasted Chicken Breast with Port Wine Sauce

Serves 4

4 boneless chicken breasts

Marinade Ingredients:
1/2 cup dry red wine
1/4 cup good quality port
1/4 cup olive oil
2 tablespoons balsamic vinegar
2 tablespoons maple syrup
2 tablespoons soy sauce
2 bay leaves
1 teaspoon fresh pepper, ground
2 garlic cloves, crushed
4 sprigs fresh thyme
1/2 teaspoon juniper berries
2 tablespoons gin

Port Sauce Ingredients:
2 pounds chicken bones
2 carrots, peeled and chopped
1 onion, diced
3 celery stalks, chopped
1 bay leaf
1/2 teaspoon dried thyme
1 garlic clove, minced
3 quarts water
1/2 cup beef stock
1 cup + 2 tablespoons port
1/2 cup olive oil
2 tablespoons butter

Continued on next page

Aspens
Aurora

1. Rinse chicken breasts under water.
2. Combine all marinade ingredients in a non-metallic bowl and whisk well. Add chicken and marinate for 2 hours at room temperature or overnight in the refrigerator.
3. To prepare Port Sauce, preheat oven to 375 degrees. Combine bones, onion, celery, carrots, bay leaf, thyme, garlic, 1 cup port and seasonings in a roasting pan and roast for 45 minutes. Transfer bones and vegetables to a stock pot and water.. Bring water to a boil, reduce to a simmer until the liquid is reduced to 1 1/2 cups. Strain the sauce and set aside.
4. Place olive oil in a sauté pan over high heat.
5. Drain the chicken breasts of marinade. Add chicken to sauté pan and cook until done. Add sauce, butter and 2 tablespoons port to the pan and cook until the sauce is glossy. Serve.

Roasted Quail with Foie Gras, Grapes au Jus, French Country Potatoes & Baby Vegetables

Serves 2

2 quail
1 ounce duck liver (foie gras)
2 spinach leaves
rosemary
olive oil as needed
3 tablespoons potatoes
2 tablespoons grapes (black and white)
2 tablespoons combined thyme, white mushrooms, shallots
2 tablespoons quail jus
basil
red wine reduction

Baby Vegetables Ingredients:
2 carrots
3 snow peas
1 cherry tomato
1 asparagus

1. Stuff spinach and foie gras in quail. Put rosemary and olive oil on top of quail before cooking. Roast at 450 degrees for 10 minutes.
2. To prepare Grapes au Jus, combine red wine reduction, quail jus, grapes, olive oil and salt and pepper to taste.
3. Cook mushrooms, thyme and shallots with olive oil.
4. Steam potatoes and mix with mushrooms and shallots. Salt and pepper to taste.
5. Steam baby vegetables.
6. Place quail, potatoes and vegetables on plate. Mix basil and olive oil together and strain around plate.

Penrose Room
Colorado Springs

Southwest Margarita Chicken Breast

8 ounces boneless chicken breast
2 tablespoons lime juice
1 tablespoon green chilis, diced (hot or mild)
1 tablespoon shallots, diced
1 tablespoon tequila
1 tablespoon triple sec
1 tablespoon olive oil

Serves 8

1. In sauté pan place olive oil and heat to medium. Place chicken breast in hot oil and cover. Cook on medium heat for 3 minutes, turn, cover and cook on other side for 3 minutes or until almost done. Uncover, add shallots, chilis and lime juice. Continue to cook over medium heat until juice is reduced by half. Add tequila and triple sec and flame until flame goes out.
2. Remove chicken breast to plate and spoon remaining ingredients over top. Garnish with slice of lime.

Best Western
Durango Inn & Suites

Café Durango
Durango

Farm House Chicken

Chicken Ingredients:
6 ounces chicken breast
1 ounce smoked ham
2 tablespoons Monterey Jack cheese
2 tablespoons Asiago cheese, coarsely grated

Serves 1

Marsala Sauce Ingredients:
1/4 cup mushrooms
2 tablespoons Marsala wine
1/4 cup demi glace
1 1/2 teaspoons shallots
1/4 cup vegetable oil

1. Divide chicken breast into (2) 3 ounce pieces. Place ham and jack cheese atop one of the breast pieces. Place second breast 3/4 of the way over top of first breast. Sprinkle Asiago over the top of the breasts. Bake at 450 degrees for 15 - 20 minutes.
2. In a small sauté pan, sauté mushrooms and shallots until tender. Add Marsala wine and demi glace. Reduce to desired consistency.
3. Remove chicken from oven and place on dinner plate. Serve with 3 ounces of Marsala Sauce and mushrooms.

Aspen Lodge Restaurant
Estes Park

Chicken Braised with Endives

1 small chicken (about 2 pounds)
1 pound endives
salt and pepper to taste
flour
2 tablespoons clarified butter
1 cup cream
1/4 lemon

Serves 2

1. Clean chicken and cut wing tips. Using poultry shears, splits the chicken open along the backbone and remove the vertebrae. Spread the chicken open and remove the small ribs and the entire breastbone, being careful not to cut through the chicken. Do not detach the two sides.
2. Season chicken with salt and pepper and dust lightly with flour. Melt the clarified butter in a heavy casserole or skillet with a cover and sauté the chicken, skin side first, until golden brown. Turn and brown the other side.
3. Cut the endives into small julienne strips. Wash and dry on paper towels. Place around the chicken, cover, and cook over low heat for 10 minutes to bring out the flavor. Add cream and bring to a boil, uncovered. Reduce to barely a simmer, re-cover and cook for 20 minutes or until done. Prick the joint of the chicken at the thigh. When chicken is done, juice should run clear and not pink.
4. Adjust seasoning with a squeeze of lemon juice and serve from the casserole.

Andre's Bistro
Vail

Desserts

Mousse au Chocolat

4 eggs
6 ounces semi-sweet chocolate
2 tablespoons hot water
2 tablespoons Grand Marnier
1 1/2 cups whipping cream
4 tablespoons powdered sugar

Serves 4

1. Separate eggs.
2. Melt chocolate and mix with egg yolks, hot water and Grand Marnier. Remove from heat.
3. Whip egg whites using whip at Speed 4 until very soft peaks form. Gradually add sugar, beating until soft peaks form. Transfer to different bowl and fold in chocolate mixture.
4. Clean bowl and whip whipped cream at Speed 4.
5. Fold chocolate mixture into whipped cream.
6. Pour into individual serving glasses or dishes.

Andre's Bistro
Avon

Sweet Tamales with Raspberries and Chocolate

masa harina (corn meal)
8 ounces cream cheese, softened
Honey
raspberry preserves
corn husks
double fudge brownie batter

Serves
8 - 10

1. In a mixer or large bowl, mix the cream cheese and honey until blended and sweet to your taste. Slowly add the masa until the mixture is crumbly. It should not be sticky. Set aside.
2. Separate the corn husks and soak in water for at least on hour until soft. For a festive alternative, color the water with red food coloring. Once soft, pat dry.
3. Make a batch of double fudge brownies with your favorite recipe (or Pillsbury works great) but do not cook the mixture.
4. Cut one corn husks into 1/4" strips to use as ties.
5. Lay out each corn husk and spread brownie mix about 1/4" thick to within 1/2" of the sides and ends. Crumble masa cream cheese mixture over brownie mixture until covered. Spread 1 teaspoon raspberry preserves on top. Roll corn husk so that the sides overlap. Take the thin strips and gently tie both ends like a package so the corn husks will not open. You now have a tamale.
6. Place tamales in a steamer basket or perforated pan over boiling water and cover. Steam for approximately 12 minutes or until firm. Remove from steamer to plate, cool, then refrigerate for at least 1 hour before serving.

Best Western
Durango Inn & Suites
Café Durango
Durango

Exquisite English Toffee Cookies

1 cup butter
1 cup packed brown sugar
1 egg
2 cups flour
1/2 cup pecan, finely chopped

Makes 48 cookies

1. Melt butter and mix well with brown sugar.
2. Separate egg.
3. Beat yolk in butter/brown sugar mixture. Add flour and mix well.
4. Pat the dough in the bottom of a jelly roll pan.
5. Beat egg white and spread over the top of the dough. Sprinkle pecans over dough and lightly pat in. Bake at 350 degrees for 30 - 35 minutes.
6. Cut immediately in 48 squares and remove from pan.

Abriendo Inn
Pueblo

Hazelnut Coffee Creme Brulee

Serves 12

1 1/2 quarts heavy cream
1 1/2 packages hazelnut coffee
pinch salt
1 1/4 cup egg yolk
3/4 cup sugar
1 1/2 tablespoons vanilla extract

1. Bring heavy cream, coffee, and salt to a simmer. Turn off heat and allow to infuse for 10 minutes. Strain and set aside.
2. Whip yolks and sugar to ribbons. Gradually add about 3/4 of the coffee cream. Pour the egg and coffee mixture back into remaining coffee cream and stir to blend in the rest by hand. Add vanilla.
3. Portion 6 ounce servings in to 12 oven proof cappuccino cups. Bake in a water bath at 325 degrees (275 degrees on a convection oven) for about 1 1/4 hours or until set.
4. Allow to chill for 4 hours before service.

Buttery Almond Toffee

1 1/4 cups unsalted butter
1 cup sugar
1/4 cup packed brown sugar
1/4 cup water
1 tablespoon water
1 cup almonds, very coarsely chopped
6 ounces bittersweet or semisweet chocolate, finely chopped or in chips
1/2 cup almonds, finely chopped

Makes 1 1/2 Pounds

1. Butter 2 baking pans.
2. Melt butter in heavy sauce pan over low heat. Add both sugars, water and honey and stir until sugar dissolves. Increase heat to medium and cook until candy thermometer registers 290 degrees, stirring slowly but constantly, scraping bottom of pan with wooden spatula for about 15 minutes. Do not stop until desired temperature is reached. As toffee finishes cooking it will froth and boil and turn amber in color.
3. Remove pan from heat. Mix in coarsely chopped nuts. Immediately pour mixture into prepared pans, being careful not to scrape the pans. Let stand 1 minute. Sprinkle with chocolate chunks and spread when softened. Sprinkle with finely chopped nuts and refrigerate until firm.
4. Break into bite-sized pieces. Chill in airtight container.

Boulder Victoria
Boulder

White Chocolate Sun-Dried Cherry Bread Pudding with Berry Sauce & Vanilla Bean Cream

Serves 12

Bread Pudding Ingredients:
2 3/4 cups 2% milk
2 3/4 cups heavy whipping cream
2 1/4 cups white sugar
4 1/4 ounces sweet butter, melted
5 eggs
2 fresh sour dough baguettes
1 pound sundried tart cherries, no pits
1 pound white chocolate chunks

Raspberry Sauce Ingredients:
1 pint fresh raspberries
1 lemon, juice of
1/2 cup sugar

Vanilla Bean Cream Ingredients:
5 egg yolks
1/2 cup white sugar
3/4 cup half & half
1 vanilla bean

Garnish:
mint leaves
fresh raspberries

1. Slice bread on an angle. Layer sliced bread in a ceramic casserole dish. Add layer of cherries and chocolate chunks and top with bread layer.
2. To prepare pudding, combine milk, cream, sugar and butter and scald over hot stove. Pour hot cream over eggs and carefully combine. Pour custard mixture over bread mass.

Continued on next page

Top of the World
Breckenridge

3. To prepare Vanilla Bean Cream, combine egg yolks and sugar over a double boiler. Scald half & half with split vanilla bean and carefully combine with egg and sugar mixture. Cook carefully and strain through a fine sieve.
4. Next, prepare Raspberry Sauce. Blend all ingredients in a food processor, strain and chill.
5. Preheat oven to 300 degrees. Cover casserole dish with aluminum foil and bake for 50 minutes. Remove foil and bake for an additional 10 minutes or until center is done.
6. Spoon a generous amount of bread pudding onto a plate, surround with vanilla cream and raspberry sauce. Garnish with fresh berries and mint leaf.

Chocolate Fondue

1 1/2 cups heavy cream
12 ounces high-quality bittersweet chocolate, finely chopped
1 tablespoon Frangelico
1 tablespoon Grand Marnier

Serves 4 - 6

1. In medium double boiler pan place chocolate and heavy cream and melt over low heat until chocolate softens. Add Frangelico and Grand Marnier and whisk until smooth.
2. Transfer to ceramic fondue pot or ceramic chafing dish and keep warm over burner.
3. Serve immediately with dipping ingredients of your choice (pound cake cut into bite-sized pieces, large fresh strawberries with stems attached, fresh cherries, banana slices, marshmallows, etc.)

The Fondue Stube
Vail

Lemon Nut Bread

1/2 cup margarine
1 1/2 cups sugar
3 eggs
2 1/4 cups flour
1/4 teaspoon salt
1/2 teaspoon baking soda
1/2 cup buttermilk
1 lemon, grated rind of
3/4 cup pecans or walnuts, chopped (optional)
2 lemons, juice of
3/4 cup powdered sugar

Makes 1 - 2 Loaves

1. Cream together margarine and sugar. Add eggs and blend well.
2. In separate bowl, combine flour, salt and baking soda.
3. Alternately add buttermilk and dry ingredients to the creamed mixture. Beginning and ending with the buttermilk. Stir in grated rind of lemon and add pecan or walnuts if desired.
4. Spoon batter into greased and floured loaf pan until 1/3 filled. Bake at 325 degrees for 1 1/4 hours or until bread tests done. Cool 15 minutes and remove from pan.
5. Combine lemon juice and powdered sugar and stir well. Punch holes in top of warm bread with toothpick. Pour on glaze. Cool on wire rack.

Elk Mountain Guest Ranch
Buena Vista

Raspberry Truffles

Makes 34 Truffles

1 cup semi-sweet chocolate chips
(2) 1 ounce squares unsweetened chocolate, chopped
1 1/2 cups powdered sugar
1/2 cup butter, softened
2 tablespoons raspberry liqueur (orange, mint or other flavors may be used)
chocolate sprinkles, cocoa, chopped nuts or cookie crumbs

1. Melt chocolate chips and unsweetened chocolate in a small heavy sauce pan over low heat, stirring constantly. Set aside and let chocolate cool.
2. Combine powdered sugar, butter, and liqueur in a bowl. Beat with electric mixer. Beat in cooled chocolate until smooth. Refrigerate for 30 minutes or until the mixture is fudgy and can be shaped into balls.
3. Shape mixture into 1" balls by rolling in the palms of your hands. Then roll truffles in chocolate sprinkles, cocoa, chopped nuts or cookie crumbs to add flavor and prevent the truffles from melting in your fingers. You can also try drizzling melted white chocolate over the plain rolled truffles for a pretty effect.

CASTLE MARNE
Denver, Colorado

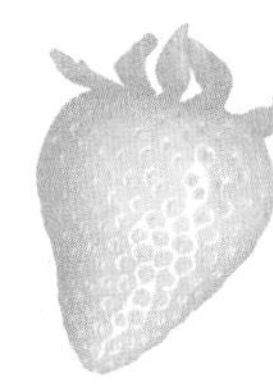

Castle Marne Bed & Breakfast
Denver

Cowboy Cookies

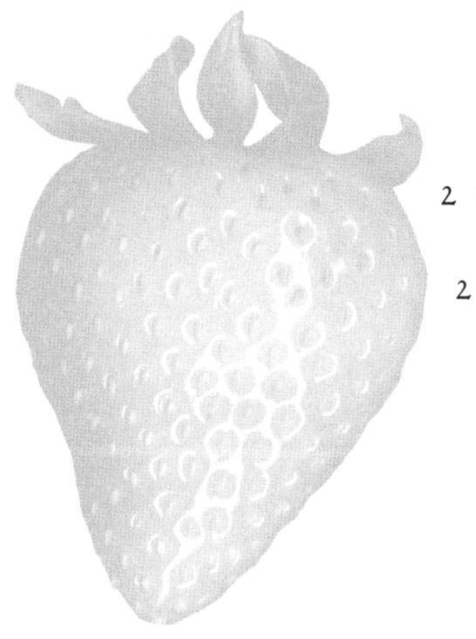

2 1/4 cups vegetable shortening
2 cups white sugar
2 1/2 cups packed brown sugar
5 eggs
3 teaspoons vanilla extract
5 cups all-purpose flour
2 teaspoons baking soda
1 teaspoon baking powder
1 teaspoon salt
3 cups dry rolled oats
2 1/2 cups corn or bran flakes
2 cups chocolate chips

Makes 4 dozen cookies

1. Cream together shortening, sugar and brown sugar. Add eggs and vanilla.
2. Sift together flour, baking soda, baking powder and salt.
3. Add dry ingredients to creamed mixture. Add oats, flakes, chocolate chips and mix well.
4. Drop rounded 1/8 cupful balls onto greased cookie sheet and bake at 325 degrees for 15 minutes or until the edges turn brown and centers still look chewy.

Alps Boulder Canyon Inn
Boulder

Peach Melba

Serves 4

Melba Sauce Ingredients:
1 pound strawberries or red raspberries
3/4 pound sugar

Peach Poaching Syrup Ingredients:
1 cup sugar
2 cups water
dash vanilla

Peaches Ingredients:
2 large peaches, peeled and pitted
whipped cream
vanilla ice cream

1. Prepare Melba. Wash berries and put in blender. Puree at Speed 2 and pass through a fine sieve. Add sugar and let stand for 1 hour, stirring occasionally.
2. To prepare poaching syrup, combine all ingredients in a sauce pan and bring to a boil. Simmer 5 minutes.
3. Drop peach halves into poaching syrup and let cook slowly for 7 - 10 minutes depending on ripeness of fruit. Remove from heat, drain and let cool.
4. To finish Peach Melba, place a scoop of ice cream into 4 large ice cream dishes. Cover with 1 peach half and pour a little Melba sauce over the peach. With a piping bag with a star tube, make a ring of cream around the peach and serve.

Andre's Bistro
Avon

Birds Nest Cookies

1/2 cup butter
1/2 cup brown sugar
1 egg, separated
speck of baking powder
1 cup flour
1 teaspoon vanilla
1/4 teaspoon almond extract
1/2 cup nuts, finely chopped

Makes 2 dozen cookies

1. Cream butter and blend in sugar. Add egg yolk, baking powder, flour and almond extract.
2. Roll in small balls and dip in unbeaten egg white. Roll in chopped nuts. Press down making hole in center.
3. Bake at 350 degrees for 10 - 12 minutes. After baking, fill hole with jelly or preserves.

Sylvan Dale Guest Ranch
Loveland

Strawberry Pie

Serves 6

1 graham cracker pie crust, 9"
16 ounces cream cheese
1/2 cup sour cream
1/2 cup powdered sugar
2 teaspoons vanilla extract
1 pint strawberries

1. Beat cream cheese and sour cream until light and fluffy. Add powdered sugar and vanilla extract and blend well.
2. Spread mixture over pie shell.
3. Cut tops off of strawberries and place in filling, tops down.
4. Refrigerate until filling sets.
5. Slice pie into 6 pieces and serve.

Radisson.
HOTEL DENVER STAPLETON PLAZA

Capers Bistro
Denver

Molten Mexican Chocolate Ecstasy

1 - 2 tablespoons butter
1/4 cup granulated sugar

1 3/4 sticks butter, softened
6 1/2 ounces Mexican chocolate*
4 eggs
4 egg yolks
1/2 cup + 1 teaspoon all-purpose flour
1 1/4 cups powdered sugar

Serves 5

*If you cannot find Mexican chocolate, substitute semi-sweet chocolate and add 1/2 teaspoon cinnamon and 1/4 teaspoon almond extract to chocolate after it is melted.

1. Preheat oven to 425 degrees.
2. Rub 4 - 5 oven proof coffee cups with butter and coat with granulated sugar, pouring excess sugar out. Set aside.
3. Chop chocolate and melt over simmering water in a double boiler. Whisk butter sticks into chocolate and then beat in eggs. Mix in flour and powdered sugar.
4. Pour enough batter into prepared cups to come 1" from the top of cup.
5. Bake for 12 - 15 minutes (the middle should be liquid) and serve warm.

Vista Verde Inn
Steamboat Springs

Les Crepes Suzettes

Serves 4

Crepe Ingredients:

4 1/2 ounces flour
4 eggs
2 tablespoons vegetable oil
1/4 cup water
1/4 cup milk
dash salt
dash sugar

Sauce Ingredients:

4 oranges, firm and juicy
4 lemons, firm and juicy
7 tablespoons granulated sugar
1/2 cup butter
6 tablespoons Grand Marnier
4 tablespoons Brandy

1. To prepare crepes, mix flour, eggs and oil together until smooth.
2. In another bowl, mix milk, water, sugar, and salt. Blend slowly into the flour mixture. You may use your blender to mix all ingredients, but let the batter stand before cooking the crepes to eliminate any excess air.
3. Oil pan before cooking the first crepe and heat over medium-high heat. Using a 2 ounce ladle, pour the batter into the pan and cook crepes one at a time.
4. In a large frying pan, melt butter over medium heat and add sugar. Zest 2 lemons and 2 oranges directly into pan, then juice all the oranges and lemons into the pan. If sugar begins to brown, stir and lower the heat if necessary. Add the liqueur, then the crepes. Let simmer in the sauce, stirring until syrupy. Spoon over the crepes, add brandy and flambé. Serve crepes on dessert plate with sauce spooned over.

Andre's Bistro
Avon

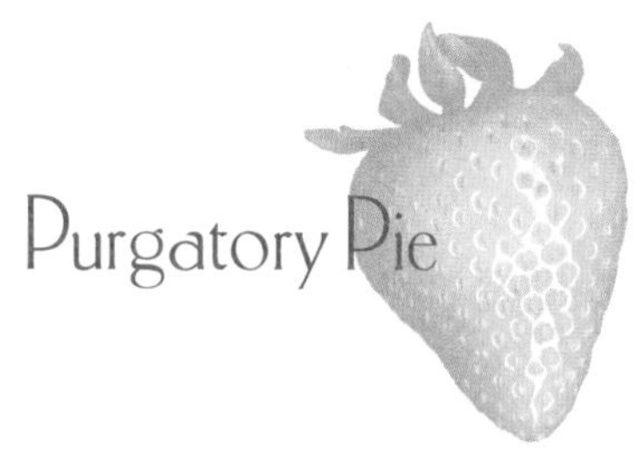

Purgatory Pie

2 unbaked pie crusts
8 ounces margarine
4 eggs
2 cups sugar
1/4 cup bourbon
1 teaspoon vanilla
1 cup flour
2 cups walnuts, chopped
1 1/2 cup chocolate chips

Makes 2 Pies

1. Melt margarine and cook to lukewarm.
2. Mix eggs and sugar to paste consistency. Add margarine, bourbon, vanilla and mix well.
3. Test temperature with finger. If mixture is cool enough, add flour. Stir in walnuts and chocolate chips.
4. Pour mixture into pie crusts.
5. Bake in convection oven with blower on at 350 degrees for 20 - 25 minutes. (Conventional oven will work also.)
6. Serve warm, topped with whipped cream.

Best Western Bent's Fort Inn
Las Animas

Ski Tip Chocolate Cake

Serves
10 - 12

Cake Ingredients:
1 3/4 cups all-purpose flour
1 teaspoon baking soda
1 teaspoon baking powder
2 1/2 tablespoons cocoa powder
10 tablespoons brown sugar
2 1/2 tablespoons corn syrup
2 eggs
2/3 cup oil
1 1/4 cup milk

Frosting Ingredients:
6 ounces sweet chocolate
2 1/2 tablespoons cream

1. Combine all cake ingredients in a mixer bowl using medium speed. Blend all ingredients thoroughly.
2. Pour into (2) 8" cake pans that have been greased and floured and bake at 350 degrees for 10 - 12 minutes. Cake is done when the top springs back.
3. Pull cake from pans and cool on rack.
4. For frosting, melt chocolate, add cream and whisk until smooth.
5. Frost top of bottom half of cake, then place top on and frost.

Ski Tip Lodge
Keystone

Kristen's Mocha Chip Cookies

2 1/2 cups semi-sweet chocolate chips
1 cup brown sugar
1 cup granulated sugar
1 cup butter, softened
2 eggs
4 teaspoons hot water
4 tablespoons instant coffee grounds
2 teaspoons vanilla
3 cups flour
1 1/2 teaspoons baking soda
1/2 teaspoon salt
powdered sugar

Makes 24 - 36 Cookies

1. Melt 1 cup of the chocolate chips over low heat and set aside.
2. Cream together butter, brown sugar and granulated sugar. Add eggs and mix until smooth.
3. Stir coffee into hot water until dissolved, then stir into the butter mixture with the vanilla. Mix in melted chocolate.
4. In a small bowl, combine flour, baking soda and salt. Gradually stir this mixture into the butter mixture. Blend in remaining chocolate chips.
5. Refrigerate dough until stiff.
6. Preheat oven to 350 degrees.
7. Form chilled dough into small balls and roll in powdered sugar. Place on ungreased cookie sheet and bake for 10 minutes. Remove from oven when surface appears "cracked" and dough has spread somewhat but not yet flat.

Boulder Victoria
Boulder

Berries Foster

Serves 2

2 tablespoons salted butter
3 tablespoons brown sugar
toasted almonds
2 cups strawberries, blueberries, raspberries, blackberries combined
1/4 cup Chambord liqueur
1/4 cup rum
2 scoops vanilla ice cream

1. In a flambé pan or a large skillet, melt butter over low heat. Add sugar and toasted almonds and mix well. Add fresh fruit to pan and sauté until they begin to soften. Pour in the liqueur and half of the rum and continue to cook over low heat.
2. Heat the remainder of the rum in a small sauce pan until it begins to boil, then quickly pour it into the flambé pan and ignite. Distribute and prolong the flame by tipping the pan with a circular motion with one hand and basting the fruit with flame, using a long-handled spoon, with the other hand. When the flame dies out serve 2 spoons of fruit to each portion and top each with a scoop of vanilla ice cream. Spoon the sauce remaining in the pan over the ice cream.

Tavern
Colorado Springs

Mystery Pecan Pie

1 unbaked pie crust
8 ounces cream cheese
1 egg
1 teaspoon vanilla
1/3 cup sugar
1 1/4 cup pecans, chopped

3 eggs
1/4 cup sugar
1 cup corn syrup
1 teaspoon vanilla

Makes 1 pie

1. Beat softened cream cheese. Add 1 egg, 1 teaspoon vanilla and 1/3 cup sugar and beat at low speed until smooth and well blended. Set aside.
2. In another bowl beat 3 eggs. Stir in 1/4 cup sugar, corn syrup and vanilla and blend well.
3. Spread cream cheese mixture in bottom of crust and sprinkle with pecans. Gently pour corn syrup mixture over pecans. Bake at 375 degrees for 40 minutes or until center is set. Cool completely before serving.

Waunita Hot Springs Ranch
Gunnison

Eagle Brand Pound Cake

Makes 1 Cake

1 pound unsalted butter
6 eggs
pinch salt
2 teaspoons vanilla
2 cups sugar
3 cups flour
1 can Eagle Brand sweetened condensed milk

1. Cream butter and sugar. Add eggs, one at a time, beating well between each. Add flour alternately with milk. Stir in vanilla.
2. Bake in well-greased and floured pan at 300 - 325 degrees for 1 1/2 hours.

Riversbend Bed & Breakfast
Mancos

Recipes by Hotel

RECIPES BY HOTEL

Abriendo Inn
300 West Abriendo Avenue
Pueblo, CO 81004
719-544-2703

Adam's Mark Hotel
1550 Court Place
Denver, CO 80202
303-893-3333

AlMar, Inc.
Allied Member
P.O. Box 261931
Littleton, CO 80163
303-346-1154

Alps Boulder Canyon Inn
38619 Boulder Canyon Drive
Boulder, CO 80302
303-444-5445

Anniversary Inn
1060 Mary's Lake Road MR
Estes Park, CO 80517
970-586-6200

Beaver Run Resort
620 Village Road
Breckenridge, CO 80424
970-453-6000

Best Western Bent's Fort Inn
P.O. Box 108
Las Animas, CO 81054
719-456-0011

Best Western Brush
1208 North Colorado Avenue
Brush, CO 80723
303-842-5146

Best Western Durango
21382 U.S. Hwy 160 West
Durango, CO 81302
970-247-3251

Best Western Executive Hotel
4411 Peoria Street
Denver, CO 80012
303-373-5730

Boulder Victoria Historic Inn
1305 Pine Street
Boulder, CO 80302
303-938-1300

Banana Sour Cream Coffee Cake 56
Buttery Almond Toffee 247
Kristen's Mocha Chip Cookies 261

Brown Palace Hotel
321 17th Street
Denver, CO 80202
303-297-3111

Braised Lobster Medallions & Sea Scallops with Roasted Red Pepper Sabayon 150
Sashimi and Guacamole Terrine with Sesame Seed Vinaigrette 78

C Lazy U Ranch
3640 CO Highway 125
Granby, CO 80446
970-887-3344

Blueberry Muffins 43
Duck with Raspberry-Pepperoncini Sauce 225
Sour Cream Coffee Cake 42
Tomato Chowder 117
Veal Stuffed with Panchetta Smoked Gouda 210

Castle Marne Bed & Breakfast
1572 Race Street
Denver, CO 80206
303-331-0621

Raspberry Truffles 252
Royal Scones 38
Teacakes 59

Copper Mountain Resort
209 Ten Mile Circle
Copper Mountain, CO 80443
970-968-2882

Grilled Trout with Fire Roasted Tomato Caper Sauce and Basil Oil 180
Pesce's Clam Chowder 118
Roasted Garlic Pesto 72

Cottonwood Inn & Gallery
123 San Juan Avenue
Alamosa, CO 81101
719-589-3882

Jennifer's Breakfast Crepes with Mexican Chocolate & Whipped Cream 24

Del Norte Motel & Café
1050 Grand Avenue
Del Norte, CO 81132
719-657-3581

Baked Bacon and Eggs 22
The I Can't Bake Chocolate Chip Banana Nut Bran Muffin 40

Denver Marriott City Center
1701 California Street
Denver, CO 80202
303-291-3603

Spinach & Wild Mushroom Strudel 144

Denver Marriott Tech Center
4900 South Syracuse
Denver, CO 80237
303-779-1100

Grilled Vegetable Panini 129

DoubleTree Hotel Denver
3202 Quebec Street
Denver, CO 80207
303-321-3333

Herb Crusted Salmon on Fresh Spinach Leaves 184

DoubleTree Hotel Durango
501 Camino Del Rio
Durango, CO 81301
970-259-6580

Grilled Filet Mignon: Mesquite Seasoned & Wrapped in Peppered Bacon with Onion Marmalade and Cheese-herb Grits 195

Elk Mountain Guest Ranch
P.O. Box 910
Buena Vista, CO 81211
719-539-4430

Cheese and Bacon in a Bread Boat 76
Eggs and Sausage Casserole 12
Lemon Nut Bread 251
Sherry's Barbeque Brisket 202

Embassy Suites Denver Downtown
1881 Curtis Street
Denver, CO 80202
303-312-3810

Carne Adovada 203
Southwestern White Pizza 65

Estes Valley Resorts
6120 Highway 7
Estes Park, CO 80517
970-586-8133

Cajun Crevettes 136
Elk Maison 201
Farm House Chicken 238
Fresh Tuna Nicoise 181
Rainbow Trout Almondine 159

Gold Lake Mountain Resort
3371 Gold Lake Road
Ward, CO 80581
303-459-3544

Campari-Lemon Granite 82
Salad of Arugula, Country Ham & Aged Goats' Cheese Vinaigrette 104
Seared Escolar with Pisaladiere Sorrel Sauce and Red Kale 178

Goldminer Hotel
601 Klondyke Avenue
Eldora, CO 80466
303-258-0226

Goldminer Muffins 18
Special Omelet 25

Grand Lake Lodge
15500 U.S. Highway 34
Grand Lake, CO 80447
970-627-3967

Cajun Linguine Pasta with Shrimp & Crawfish Tails 132
Pan Seared Filet Medallions on a bed of Caramelized Onions with a Balsamic Glaze 206

Holden House 1902 B&B
1102 West Pikes Peak Avenue
Colorado Springs, CO 80904
719-471-3980

German Puff Pancakes with Spiced Apples 48
Ruffled Crepes Isabel 28
South Western Eggs Fiesta 11

Holiday Inn Denver Southeast
3200 South Parker Road
Aurora, CO 80014
303-695-1700

Hot Springs Lodge & Pool
401 North River Road
Glenwood Springs, CO 81602
970-945-2846

Hotel Colorado
526 Pine Street
Glenwood Springs, CO 81601
970-945-6511

Hotel Jerome
330 East Main Street
Aspen, CO 81611
970-920-1000

Hyatt Regency Beaver Creek
50 West Thomas Place
Beaver Creek, CO 81620
970-949-1234

Hyatt Regency Denver Tech Center
7800 East Tufts Avenue
Denver, CO 80237
303-779-1234

Hyatt Regency Denver Downtown
1750 Welton Street
Denver, CO 80202
303-295-1234

Inverness Hotel & Golf Club
200 Inverness Drive West
Englewood, CO 80112
303-799-5800

Keystone Resort
P.O. Box 38
Keystone, CO 80435
303-496-4226

Corn Chutney 99
Forest Mushroom with Goat's Beard 84
Garden Room Caesar Dressing 95
Rack of Lamb Chops with Oven Roasted Vegetables 216
Roast Breast of Chicken with Focaccia Lemon Sage Stuffing 227
Ski Tip Chocolate Cake 260
Stubé Greens 90
Stubé Pine Cone Paté 77

Latigo Ranch
201 Country Road 1911
Kremmling, CO 80459
970-724-9008

Chicken and Artichoke 224
Poppy Seed Sour Cream Potatoes 142
Spinach Balls 88

Loews Giorgio
4150 East Mississippi Avenue
Denver, CO 80222
303-782-9300

Golden Gazpacho 123
Hazelnut Coffee Creme Brulee 246
Red Pepper Soup 110
Seafood Stew 108

Logwood Bed & Breakfast
35060 U.S. Highway 550 North
Durango, CO 81301
970-259-4396

Breakfast Casserole 45
Green Chicken Enchilada Casserole 17
Pumpkin Bread 37

Manor Vail Lodge
595 East Vail Valley Drive
Vail, CO 81657
970-476-5000

Sesame Crusted Mahi-Mahi with Tomato Wasabi Vinaigrette 169

Mount Elbert Lodge
10764 Highway 82
Twin Lakes, CO 81251
719-486-0594

Mt. Elbert Rhubarb Muffins 41
Upside Down Muffin Pie 57

North Fork Guest Ranch
P.O. Box B
Shawnee, CO 80475
303-838-9873

Blueberry Smoothie 46
Blueberry Streusel Cake 34
Colorado Pine Nut Salad 102

Old Town GuestHouse
115 South 26th Street
Colorado Springs, CO 80904
719-623-9194

Crumb Coffee Cake 44
Curry Cheese Paté 83
Yeast-Raised Pancakes 53

Hotel	Recipes
Strater Hotel 699 Main Street Durango, CO 81301 970-247-4431	Filet Herbert 194 Pasta Pescotore 134
Sylvan Dale Guest Ranch 2939 North County Road 31D Loveland, CO 80538 970-667-3915	Artichoke Heart Dip 64 Birds Nest Cookies 255 Tillie's Granola 23
Table Mountain Inn 1310 Washington Avenue Golden, CO 80401 303-277-9898	Anaheim Chicken Salad 101 Mesquite Grilled Salmon over Yellow Pepper Coulis with a Tomato & Cucumber Slaw 186
The Baldpate Inn 4900 South Highway 7 Estes Park, CO 80517 970-586-6151	Apple Apricot Salad 100 Banana Butterscotch Muffins 26 Key-sch Supreme 55
The Black Forest B&B 11170 Black Forest Road Colorado Springs, CO 80908 719-495-4208	Morning Glory Muffins 16
The Broadmoor One Lake Avenue Colorado Springs, CO 80901 719-634-7711	Berries Foster 262 Chicken Piccata with Lemon Caper Butter Sauce 226 Colorado Free Range Venison with Blue Cheese and Foie Gras Souffle in Hazelnut Game Jus 196 Crispy Filet of Colorado Brook Trout with Saffron Mussel Chowder 174 Grilled Tournedos of Swordfish with Fresh Herb Salade & Mousseline Potatoes 155 Mountain Honey & Cumin Roasted Colorado Rack of Lamb with Sweet Garlic Rosemary Jus 209 Roasted Quail with Foie Gras, Grapes au Jus, French Country Ptatoes & Baby Vegetables 236 Strawberry Soup 115 Tavern Garden Burger 143
The Chateau at Vail 13 Vail Road Vail, CO 81657 970-476-5631	Chocolate Fondue 250

The Christie Lodge
0047 East Beaver Creek Blvd.
Avon, CO 81620
970-949-7700

Breast of Chicken with Morel Mushrooms & Cream 233
Chicken Braised with Endives 239
Les Crepes Suzettes 258
Mousse au Chocolat 243
Peach Melba 254

The Lodge & Spa at Breckenridge
112 Overlook Drive
Breckenridge, CO 80424
970-453-9300

Bruschetta with Goat Cheese & Tapenade 73
Grilled Filet of Atlantic Salon with Chive Sauce Presented with Cream Leeks & Asparagus 182
Traditional Spanish Paella 172
White Chocolate Sun-Dried Cherry Bread Pudding with Berry Sauce & Vanilla Bean Cream 248

The Lodge & Spa at Cordillera
2205 Cordillera Way
Edwards, CO 81632
970-926-2200

Red Deer Mignon with Ginger & Lemon Broccoli Mousseline 200

The Lodge at Vail
174 East Gore Creek Road
Vail, CO 81657
970-476-5011

Colorado Corn Risotto 139
Grilled Colorado Lamb T-bone with Butternut Squash, Cinnamon-Cap Mushrooms & Potato Gnocch 212
Grilled Honey Marinated Squab Breast 228

The Oxford Hotel
1600 17th Street
Denver, CO 80202
303-628-5400

Crab Stuffed Mushrooms 89
Fresh Tuna Nicoise 97
Sole Parmesan 158

The Peaks Resort & Spa
136 Country Club
Telluride, CO 81435
970-728-6800

Cantaloupe Gazpacho 122
Diver Scallops with Udon Noodles 154

The Silvertree Hotel
100 Elbert Lane
Snowmass Village, CO 81615
970-923-3520

Grilled Lamb with Tomato Pearl Cous Cous 218
Grilled Slamon Roulade with Aioli 149
Shrimp and Scallop Thai Pasta 128

The Stonebridge Inn
300 Carriage Way
Snowmass Village, CO 81615
970-923-2420

Grilled Lemon Marinated Swordfish with Roasted Red Pepper Remoulade 166
Raspberry Vinaigrette 92

Index

A

B

E

F

G

H

T

U

V

W

Order Form

Fax orders: (303) 297-8104

Telephone orders: Call (303) 297-8335

On-line orders: www.coloradolodging.com

Postal orders: Colorado Hotel & Lodging Association
999-18th Street, Suite 1240
Denver, CO 80202

E-mail orders: martini@chla.com

Please send ______ copies of

INNcredible Edibles
Recipes from Colorado's Hotel Chefs

@ $19.99 per copy.

Please add 7.3% sales tax for books shipped to Colorado addresses.
Shipping cost is $5.00 for the first book and $3.00 for each additional book.

Total amount due: $________________

Payment (circle one):

Check

Credit Card

Visa
MasterCard
American Express

Card number: ____

Expiration date: ____________________

Name on card: ____

Signature: ____

I understand that I may return any books for a full refund, for any reason, no questions asked.

ORDER NOW!